American Lambs

*Poems and Stories about Working
Border Collies, Sheep, Family,
and Life on the Land*

T Yamamoto

Cover photograph taken on Waupoos Island, courtesy of Harinui Farm, www.harinuifarm.ca.

ISBN-13: 978-0-9794690-5-3
ISBN-10: 0-9794690-5-8

Library of Congress Control Number: 2009937443

Dedication

To farmers, ranchers and conservationists who are trying to find a balance. And to my husband, Pete. A good man and a farmer.

8

Author's Note

These stories and poems are made up of fiction, myth, and reality from my family, friends, and my own life. The timeline in the book is not quite linear.

Bush Island is not a real place. But it is based on a real island off the coast of the Pacific Northwest.

Like all beautiful rural communities, this place was first agricultural. Then, very slowly, the populace and the landscape changed.

The farming families began to sell their land as taxes went up and the new population didn't realize that they were changing the exact things they loved about the island.

My husband's family are fourth-generation farmers from around this region.

All their land is now gone.

Contents

Morning

I wake up to the sun peeking behind the tall firs into our bedroom window. A little breeze wraps around my legs as I go get firewood.

My Pete makes coffee, and then eats breakfast: lamb chops, goat milk in my coffee, nothing in his. He goes out to do his wildlife chores.

I pull on my tall boots; the mud is deep next to the barn. The dogs know exactly what time to meet me at the door to go out and start feeding.

The little black pup, Sweep the Broom, whines a bit as he knows he isn't allowed down to stock yet.

This makes the sled team bark.

The dogs frisk about my legs as I walk out to feed my stock horses first. They watch me in the way wise old horses do. I toss in a few flakes and note that my neighbor's hay is better this year.

Then I walk out to the flock of rams and toss some hay in to them. They are a thin group after breeding season. One ram stomps at the dogs. Gunny freezes and stalks up close and thinks about what she'd like to do. Little Cap sits down a few yards away. I watch the Cap's face and wonder what he is thinking, probably, "Why irritate the old bastard ram, just leave him be."

I go down the driveway and the tops of the firs sway in the southwest wind, the wind that brings rain.

I toss hay to my filly, stationed down there with the ewes, and look over the sheep and their lambs. They are quiet and regard me with calm awareness. But they start up towards the tall gate because they know I will trail them up a few miles to another pasture today.

I open the gate and my dogs slip through and Cap, wiser, goes directly to the back of the field to look in the hiding places for any sheep reluctant to join the flock. Gunny brings up the sheep that are closest, as always, eager and too quick, I tell her easy, easy and she gives me a quick look.

I decide to walk. The sheep know this drill and follow me willingly with the dogs behind them, and we walk down the old dirt road and turn and head north through the deep woods. The sheep are quiet except for the sound of their hooves. Cap stays well back but Gunny has to be reminded that this is not a race.

The trees wave above us and I wonder if this is what being at the bottom of the sea is like.

Clouds scud overhead and the sunlight is dim. It is damp and cold and I zip up my jacket.

My walking has a rhythm, the sheep and dogs have a rhythm, and it is old and comforting. I see tracks in the mud of other travelers through the forest.

We reach the logging road and the sheep spread out. This makes Gunny excited and she flops back and forth till I turn and tell her to easy and she begins to realize that she can hold the sheep from farther back.

The four old ewes that are belled trot along and their bells ring lightly. The sky opens up and a light rain begins to fall. We come to a clear cut area and the trees reach up all around it like a cathedral, they are so tall.

We puff up a hill and the ewes slow. Cap pushes lightly from the back, nonchalantly, innocently.

We turn and head down a ravine and the trees close in again. Here and there like fallen dinosaurs are great old giants that fell during the '06 storm. Their root balls huge and profound, out of the earth where they were torn.

Then back on a gravel road. I down the dogs and stop. The old ewes stop beside me. I look for cars. But there is no one. We go on.

We pass a cabin with a For Sale sign and a mother and two kids come out to wave. Cap, even though he knows he is not allowed, goes up to say hello, and I call him after he has his little pat from the children's hands.

"Want coffee?" the mother calls. "On the return!" I answer.

I know those kids, their mother, where she works, where her husband lives now, why the house is for sale.

The dogs only know they like the kids. Although Gunny is shy.

We turn off onto another trail and through one little meadow. The grass is still pretty good here. But my neighbors and I need to get rid of the tansy. We go on and the sun is shining again and I can see far to the mountains with a lace of snow on their shoulders.

I open the gate and the ewe flock walks inside and my dogs lay down. I check the water and the fenceline.

I think of my childhood and realize this is a great gift.

And this is my day off.

I turn, call the dogs, and walk home.

Moving Day

The farm house is 100 years old.

Creaky floors, dust that floats down from someone's footsteps upstairs.

The lumber to build it

Hand sawn, cross marks like the ripples in mud at low tide.

Ancient trees.

Now, not even re-used.

The double-handled saw is in our tool room.

The house sits on a city lot that once was hundreds of acres of farmland.

The old woman is 95.

She was born in this house, raised her kids here.

They were taken from this house and interred, but got it back because farmers stuck together no matter what color you were.

Native, Japanese, Italian or Swede.

Her husband died here.

She takes very little away, only memories that are heavy and sweet.

The bulldozer moves earth.

And a car dealership waits.

A man from Scotland adopted this family many years ago.

As he and his wife had no children.

The only legacy he has now is a great grandchild that plays the pipes.

And the Bush Island sheep I browse.

Thanksgiving

———————•———————

"What are you doing?"

"Trimming . . ."

"Hum?" The old man leans down and inspects a ewe's foot.

"Why are you trimming?"

"Grandpa, I'm trimming because the ewe's hoof is too long. And she is starting some infection right here." I point with the hoof knife.

Grandpa straightens up and looks at me funny.

"You are not walking them far enough."

§§§

The hoof knife sits rusty on the windowsill overlooking the dog yard where the dogs sleep and wait for sheep.

"Who was that guy then?"

"That was the hay man."

"Hum? What he set you back then?"

"A lot, Grandpa."

Grandpa raises his eyebrows so high they almost disappear into his iron grey hair.

He goes over and fingers some brush next to the dirt road. It is salal, and evergreen huckleberry mostly, some small Doug fir saplings. He fingers them and looks at me.

He says nothing, just that quizzical Grandpa look. Then he stumps away.

I test the old Bush Island ewes on the brush. They eat with great relish. I take out the entire flock and the more civilized sheep go right to the grass. I browse the flock on the ever-green brush for seven years. Sheep that do well, I keep; sheep that don't, I cull.

§§§

My hay bill goes way down.

The browsing takes time, but I write more poetry.

My ewes are fat, I am thinner.

My dogs are calm.

§§§

We are shearing.

My feet are slipping on the board and a ewe's horns are poking me. I am doing this by hand and the young man who is catching for me is slow, as this is his first time. The dogs corner a ewe in the paddock and he uses the leg crook, upends with a groan and pulls her to me as I release the first one, who bounds away like an antelope. I am an indifferent shearer, and the ewe shows this by the patterns on her body.

After all the sheep are done we bring open bags of wool into the cabin and stack them neatly in our storage room.

Grandpa is sitting looking at an oil painting I was working on.

He then glances at Great Grandma's wheel sitting, dusty, in the place we put things to be fixed.

"How much does it cost to frame the painting?"

"A lot, Grandpa."

"How much the oil paint?"

I shrug; I know where this is going.

Grandpa gets up, he walks to the wool room, he comes back, three swatches of different-colored wool in his dark hands. He holds them up to the painting, here and there. He points at the spinning wheel and gives me his look of disapproval.

"Your grandmother made paintings."

He stumps away and goes to look at a pot, simmering sheep's milk for cheese, on the stove.

My shearing improves.

We are sitting on the bed. It is a warm day. We are watching dogs running sheep on the TV

Grandpa is squinting through glasses. His breath is wheezy.

The sheepdogs are watching too.

"I know what your problem is with your dogs."

"What's that, Grandpa?"

"You talk too loud and too much."

"Ok, then."

§§§

The county calls me.

She asks me to come teach how to brain tan hides and render fat and make soap for their agriculture classes.

I say I will.

I turn and look at Grandpa's picture on the refrigerator.

"Thanks, old man." I tell him.

Then very softly to the dogs, "Here."

We go outside to browse the sheep.

Pete

He is chopping wood.

He is using the old maul that remembers my family's grip.

The wood is from the tumbled trees that fell in '06.

He smiles at me as I watch.

My hands are damp from dishes.

No kids are here to see.

His eyes are smiling. He thinks of his chores.

I look at the rounds of wood. That one fell in the dark, near where we were standing; we couldn't hear it as the chainsaw drowned out even the roar of eighty-mile-per-hour winds.

We decided that night.

We were partners. Old Time Husband and Wife as my relatives might have put it.

That night he ran one way to check the rams and little horses, I ran down the other, to the ewe flock, branches hitting me as the dark screamed by. The dogs, close, tails down, ears back. One yelped as a branch struck a glancing blow.

The ewe flock were standing facing the back of the wind. My flashlight jumped over them, flashing green from their eyes. I looked up to the tortured trees, then consigned the ewe's fate to creation and turned and ran back.

We woke from trembling timid sleep into a changed world. Barn flat, trucks crushed, but ewes untouched . . . ancient trees that now leaned on the cabin, whose homemade roof had held our lives.

The dogs smiled in the morning, and wagged their tails, licked our hands.

Pete went out and chain sawed rounds and split wood to burn in the wood stove that keeps us warm.

Spirit

It took all his energy that day.

That ghost that pushed his way through one world into this one.

And as I despaired about life and my place in it, unable to find balance or teach it,

This wise invisible ghost whispered loudly in my ear.

And through that word

I was able to teach and be taught.

To take life and help bring it into the world.

I was fed and did feed.

I unclothed and made cloth.

And my partners were a tired horse from the rez, two rescued dogs. (One that wouldn't head.)

My husband and a menagerie of wildlife and kids from all over the world.

And that simple nomad ghost

He whispered one word

Sheep.

Just Past the Roy Y

(On the way to the horse vet, I left this note on a telephone pole.)

You didn't have a collar

You and your friend were headed west.

Had you worked sheep?

Your pads hard and rough,

Straw in your coats.

What happened, little dogs?

Where were you running from?

Where were you running to?

One with a crooked blaze

One with a bald face.

Car hit one of you.

In the middle of the two-lane highway,

You lay on the double yellow line.

Your friend had gone back to your side

And was hit as well.

§§§

What do people see as they pass?

Woman dragging dead dogs off the road.

One guy honks his red truck horn at me.

What do they see?

A guy stops.

He is pulling an empty stock trailer.

His living dog glances at my living dogs, through one window into another, then out at us.

We look at our dogs, then a resolute unwavering meeting of our eyes.

The man says nothing.

Gets out a shovel from the back of his pickup.

He helps me drag the dogs to the edge of the forest.

He digs a hole.

We put the dogs in, side by side.

Two black-and-white sheepdogs.

Like ours.

I have a wool bag in my truck.

I get out two pieces of wool and drop it down

And it floats soft to land nesting on the top of the dogs.

We say nothing.

The man takes off his hat and goes back to his truck and drives off.

What do they see, the people who drive past?

I get back into my truck

I pat my dogs.

I know what that man and I saw.

A good partner

Long dead.

The Bull Dog

My great uncle killed a man in a fight in a bar in War Eagle and fled to Canada.

He changed his name; the family said he was the black sheep.

He wandered and never married, just him and his dog.

Tall, old, slick-coated dog who could find stock or rabbits.

My uncle got work at a dairy farm, so the story goes.

These were in the days when a farm kept their own bull.

One day a tourist climbed in to see what beast was kept behind such a fence.

Sometimes curiosity is not such a good thing.

My uncle saw the man get tossed by the bull. And him and his dog jumped the rails.

Dog grabbed the bull by the nose and hung on while my great uncle whipped off his jacket and beat the bull about the face.

The whole mess circled round the paddock, the dairyman ran to get his gun.

The tourist escaped with a broken arm.

The bull finally ran back into his stall.

My uncle survived.

The family said, "A life for a life."

But . . .

They only invited the dog back.

Teaching

The boy knelt over a sheep pelt. He was gingerly rubbing sheep brains into the flesh side.

"Didn't think you'd ever do this . . . huh?" I asked him.

He shook his dark head, afro wobbling merrily.

"See, if you do this and then smoke it, it will stay soft. And if it gets wet it won't get hard again like rawhide. My grandpa taught me how."

The boy gave me a sidelong glance. This boy was from New York City. His parents moved to this remote place because of what they witnessed during 9/11.

"If your grandpa wanted a rug, he could have gone to K-mart. How long do I rub this?"

"Till it's dry."

I knelt down by him. "Why do you come help me?"

"My dad makes me."

"Oh."

§§§

The boy held the sheep between his legs. The ewe lamb was kicking, because she was uncomfortable and he had just nicked her flank with the hand shears.

"Look, Tea, I saw that people do this really quickly on the Internet, man, it takes them a minute. Don't you have electric shears?"

"What's your hurry?"

"Why is she kicking?"

"She's uncomfortable. Roll her so she's kind of on the side of her quarters."

"How do you have the patience to do this?"

"What else is there to do?"

He groans.

§§§

"Squeeze harder."

"Uh . . . nothing is happening."

"You're not squeezing right."

"This is so weird; it's like the Nature Channel. Ever watch it?"

"I have my own Nature Channel, called The Project."

"Nothing is happening; hey look . . . a drop of milk! WOW, it's really coming out now!"

I stand up from crouching next to the boy, milking my goat.

"This is what we BUY at the store," he tells me.

§§§

"What are you doing?"

"I'm putting her down."

"Why! Don't! She doesn't want to die."

"Most things don't, she's suffering and I'm her shepherd and it's her time. So I'm helping her."

The boy walks away, turns and gives me an angry, sad, defiant glance.

Soon she is gone.

The boy slowly walks back. Almost as if against his will.

"Now what are you doing?"

"I'm going to skin her and field dress her. I won't let her go to waste."

A long pause.

"That's like the meat at the store. The meat is from a living thing."

"Yes, it is."

His eyes reveal a great truth finally realized.

§§§

Years later.

A note comes in the mail.

Tea and Pete,

I just want to say, thank you.

I look at the return address, a strange postmark and stamp and "Peace Corps" written on it.

From Uganda.

The Mean Ram

The horned ram had hit me and his 250 pounds knocked me flat.

I looked up to see his golden-eyed gaze, calm, serene, and he charged and I rolled out of the way.

I yelled at him.

And my poor young bitch ran off, thinking it was her fault.

I wondered what would happen if he hit me in the head?

He charged again.

He saw wolves eating his wives . . .

Lions eating his lambs.

I sprawled out of his way, grabbed wool and twisted him off his devil's feet.

The bitch came back and apologized to me by gripping him between the eyes till I could get to my feet and pick up a fallen branch.

We penned him and I went to get a rifle.

The bitch went and hid but my old dog came with me.

I told the ram

You are right not to trust us.

And I will always keep one of your sons.

Because it is your spirit that kept the loose dog from killing my flock, your daughters.

But you need to either come back a wild mountain sheep

Or remember your shepherd.

He looked at me out of those calm golden eyes

And stomped his front foot.

I was surprised that I could not shoot him.

And instead turned him loose in the hills to run with the wild sheep

To breed lambs that are strong and wise and fearless.

Banana-Eating Sheep

What is the old shepherd's saying?

If you name them they are too fat.

Banana-Eating Sheep.

That is her name.

Out of a wild horned Bush Island ewe.

By my evil ram.

Banana-Eating Sheep got a name

When as a lamb she approached her shepherd on tiny split hooves and walked past the sheepdogs that politely looked the other way. She came up to beg a bite or two of lunch while I sat in a meadow browsing her flock.

She likes bananas in particular and later if you on the hill would call out . . .

Banana-Eating Sheep! Banana-Eating Sheep! She would come at a gallop, fleece flying, and ears up.

Truly she amused us with her joy in bananas.

We would be working on the barn roof and someone would call out . . .

And soon this old white ewe would come at a gallop.

But we told the kids they must have a banana ready.

Her children, beautiful and wild.

Grandpa said it skips a generation.

Cap and Gunny

Little Cap, white with the colorful and pirate-like ears.

You taught me to be soft and slow.

You taught me diplomacy with an angry ewe.

I saw you get nailed by a ram against a Doug fir tree.

And come back to hit the ram carefully from the back.

At first I thought you weak.

Then I noticed that you are thinking and generous of your charges.

So careful of young lambs.

You are a sheepdog.

But

I run you with my falconry hawks.

Never say Rabbit around Old Cap.

You helped me track a black bear.

You helped me catch a hurt fawn.

When I am wrong you would sit down and regard me with a quizzical good humor until I figured out what you thought.

You once chased off a loose dog while we were browsing.

Gunny held the flock together and you, little dog, hair erect, on tiptoe, stalked up so the dog saw that he was trespassing and should leave at once.

Which the dog did.

Oh, Cap is like me I guess.

Gunny is a red marine.

She is guts and glory, hell bound; nothing will go against her will.

She is the one to stand down the toughest ram and most ornery ewe.

She gives cows a glare that would freeze Satan himself.

And, gentled, her gaze will get her through the gates of heaven.

Not much questions her twice.

Oh but she makes stock nervous and I have to remind her that the sheep need space.

She taught me what it means to be truly brave.

A 35-pound dog and a 1,000-pound steer.

She saved old Cap once

When a ram put him up against a tree and started to come at him again.

She left her side of the flock and leaving me gaping

Went and wrung the ram out like a dishrag.

I don't trust her completely with the lambs as I see, deep down, she feels that we need to eat them.

(A thought and process that makes Cap hide in anguish.)

Gunny was at the dog pound.

I bet someone got her from a ranch and thinking they were bringing home Babe, found that they had brought home a whole division of marines wrapped up in a little brown dog.

A border collie rescue picked her up. And called me as they knew I needed another dog.

We took her to a sheepdog clinic. I had never seen one.

Gunny knew her job at once.

She sleeps near us at night.

I see her watch me, as if not truly believing her luck.

She is like me.

Two Conversations

Cap: "Now then my dear ewe, what a nice lamb . . . Oh, what's that over there? I will look this way for a moment."

Ewe: "You demon! Touch my lamb and I will toss you as high as that grey horse."

Cap: "Now, now mother, I think Tea is feeding? Ah yes there she is . . . Hum . . . what's that over this other way? I will just walk over here, just a couple of steps and see."

Ewe: "Lamb, get back . . . dog . . . two more steps and you are going to be seeing stars."

Cap: "What a beautiful morning, ho, hum . . . Well now, Tea is feeding. Oh yes and it's the new hay . . ."

Ewe: "Really? The new hay? Lamb, get in front of me. Are you mine, lamb? Let's check . . . oh yes, you are. Well, I'm going to start over there, dog, you try anything and you'll be so sorry. Come lamb."

Cap (yawns): "Really my dear, wouldn't dream of it. I do need to go that way though. The gate is that way so I will follow, but back here. Ok . . . ?"

Ewe: "NEW HAY! Come lamb!"

§§§

Gunny: "You, ram! Son of a bitch, try that again and you'll be a meal to remember."

Ram: "Yes. I heard that before from the white dog, right after I knocked him flying."

Gunny: "I remember. He is my partner . . . you sorry sack of wool! Oh . . . let's see where I should grab ahold . . . your nose? Looks soft and tender . . . Hum? Your cheek—you need a little less wool there anyway."

Ram: "I see my friend over there; I am going over there to him."

Gunny: "Good idea. And move sharp while you're at it. I'm hungry and I have stuff to do."

The Life of My Socks

My socks were once salal and evergreen huckleberry that grow on the edges of a deep wood.

They were once salt grass growing within view of a snow capped peak where glaciers winked in new day sunshine.

My socks were the soft gurgling bleat of a mother ewe and the high wail of a black lamb with a quick tail.

Both my socks know the joy of springing up all four split feet in the air and kicking out at an imaginary predator to find only old Cap behind them.

My socks grew over the course of a summer and old flowers brushed them and rocks crushed by the slow sprawl of glaciers from centuries ago.

My socks once knew the touch of sharp steel and the hot water and soap made from relatives.

They were turned round and round on the carder and sung joyfully at my wheel while I sat at the farmers market and watched the world.

Gunny sitting under my chair.

My socks knew quiet nights as yarn as I knitted them and taught others.

They know my tired old feet, cold no longer.

My socks walk the trails with the ewe flock and their original owner now only a memory walks again on soft grass and watches her family's leaping games.

They have a history, a memory.

They are truly clothing.

The old people thought everything made with love was alive.

This I believe.

God and His Sheepdog

My young niece and I went to church because my neighbor said,

"Tea, at least expose her to religion."

(I had exposed her, but the religion was not inside.)

At church the pastor made a stirring talk about God as the good Shepherd.

(He had heard that sheep people were coming, I suppose.)

At the end when he was saying goodbye to his flock

He said to my niece, a skinny little red-cheeked thing with dark eyes like obsidian chips and sometimes as hard,

"Now I hear you folks keep sheep."

My niece nodded gravely, then stated,

"If God is a good shepherd he must have one hell of a dog."

The pastor went very still.

As still as Gunny lying down, watching a big stubborn ram.

My niece then added, "I bet God favors a big dog, 'bout nine feet tall, all black with maybe a little bit of white, a slick-coated, prick-eared dog, that right?"

The pastor didn't answer but his eyes met mine.

One of my friends then told my niece

"That's right, honey, a big old black slick-coated prick-eared dog. God's got a lot of different kinds of sheep and they are tough as stumps, and don't flock well."

My niece nodded in understanding then said quietly to me as we walked away,

"Tea, about God's dog, I guess his name is Michael . . .

But I bet God calls him Mike."

Mike, God's Dog, and
The Money-Changers

My niece at nine years old

Got stuck on the idea of God having a dog.

In fact that's what made her tag along with her cousins to church.

This provided some entertainment

As this child speculated on situations that to her must have involved

The Sheepdog of God, Mike.

When this little girl heard of Christ and the money-changers,

She assumed, rightly some thought,

That Christ, being a son of the Good Shepherd, was of course a Shepherd himself.

And his nickname was Lamb.

Well, my niece recounted this story of the money-changers, overheard by her grandmother while she was preaching to some little friends.

Well, Lamb went to town one day to sell some feeder lambs he had.

And they were top-notch lambs. All uniform with matching markings and tiny perfect horns.

White as snow in sunlight. Heck, the glare from these lambs would cause people to shield their eyes.

When Lamb got to the Market, He set up shop.

He was helped in all this by his Father's dog, Mike. A great big black, slick-coated prick-eared dog, that nothing would challenge.

Heck, this dog would round up hail in the sky on a stormy day just for fun. Or jump in the sea and shed off whales as a little practice.

So Lamb set up and proceeded to sell his sheep for a fair price. He would later give all this money, it was gold, to the food bank, and any extra lambs he would give to the poor for starter flocks.

There were merchants there at the market that were changing money.

I think it meant they were having you give them money to keep and then they gave you back money that was worthless.

Lamb heard about this and went over to look, with Mike behind his right leg. Lamb was holding a shepherd's crook made out of lightning topped with a ram's horn from his Father's flock.

He saw these folks cheating people out of their hard-earned money. And it made him so mad that the sun went out behind a bank of storm clouds. And down at the harbor the waves came in so rough that ten pirates got seasick.

He sent Mike on down to them. And Mike that big old black slick-haired prick-eared dog got down on his belly and crept up to them like they were a flock of tough horned rams that had gotten into someone's garden.

The money-changers all crept together and clutched their belongings. Some of them went to grab the money left on their tables, but Mike sent them back in a hurry with one glare from his amber eyes.

Mike rounded them up and according to Lamb's wishes Mike herded them down to the food bank where they had to cook soup and make bread all day for 1,000 years. Mike made them go at a good pace, but made sure they weren't too out of breath.

Mike shed off the worst one. And this man was tricky, trying his best to get back to his flock of money-changers for protection. But Mike could read his thoughts and out-maneuvered him on every turn. And he was sent to the goat dairy and he had to muck out the deep littered jugs forever, but they gave him free milk to drink so he wouldn't starve.

So don't forget God has a son named Lamb, and free use of his Pop's dog, Mike.

And it isn't good to exchange money, good for bad.

Great Uncle Sees the Light

One of my great uncles, whom I won't name

Had a still

For purposes of a medicinal nature

So he claims.

One day he was minding this contraption, set up in the deep woods.

Checked the mash and the copper tubing.

Earlier that day he had been reproached by his great-grand-niece on his still. Her grandmother, his sister, thought it was very bad.

The little girl told him that God was watching and if he wasn't careful, he would send Mike the Sheepdog down from a thunderhead and then he'd be sorry.

Well the story goes like this.

My uncle decided to sit down and drink a bit of his brew,

It being a fine day.

And he was out of earshot of his hardworking better half, and his dry town sister

So he sat on the stump of a snag and took sips of drink out of a mason jar. The stuff was clear as lake ice and as heavy as syrup.

When all of a sudden there above him on the hill appears a big black dog.

My uncle scolds it.

"Git out . . . Damn dog . . . go home."

Then he notices something.

It's a big black, prick-eared slick-coated dog.

No collar on it.

It stares at him with amber eyes and begins to creep down the hill.

My uncle stands up in a hurry and spills the home brew in a wide arc down his pants.

The dog is staring my great uncle in the eyes as it creeps on in.

And my uncle being a bit spiffed

Decides maybe out of the mouth of babes, maybe God's dog Mike is after him for sinning by drinking so much.

He turns tail and runs like a wild Bush Island ewe.

Runs home glancing back over his shoulder, tripping on roots and snags.

He sees the dog at times.

Not too close so it doesn't spook him over a cliff

But close enough to herd him away from the engine of evil.

When he gets to our cabin, by the reek of him we know where he's been.

We sit him down and listen to his close call with this black dog.

My grandpa begins laughing so hard he starts wiping his eyes and has to go outside.

My niece stands there arms folded across her chest like an old-time, hell-fire preacher and says

Well I told you.

Later on that day I get a phone call from my brother.

He's looking for his sheepdog, a new one he bought in BC.

It is a big black dog

With a slick coat and prick ears.

Hum, my poor great uncle.

I have a feeling he will be seeing God's dog again.

That brother's far pasture is right next to the woods that hide the still.

Dark to Light

The power is down

And I can't start the generator.

Pete is on the mainland

And the wind is coming up.

Darkness falls.

My niece and I are in the little cabin

The wonder of day and night.

All we hear is the wind in tall trees that we cannot see, only hear as a rushing and power.

It makes me nervous.

We eat our dinner next to the trustworthy woodstove that squats content on the floor boards.

Lamb stew, smoking and rich.

Sheepdogs jerk and dream on the cabin floor

My niece sits in my great aunt's chair wearing my musher's head lamp.

She tells me this,

"Grandpa told me God's sheep dog is Coyote Old Man, and he taught the mother of all sheepdogs how to move stock."

She meets my eyes

"And Runner told me God's dog was the Wolf. And he culls the deer and elk, and caribou the way we cull the sheep flock. And Great Uncle Toru said that Buddha had a beautiful flower that helped sheep. Which is true?"

I shake my head. "I don't know . . . little girl."

She looks out the window into the darkness.

"If a bear comes, will you know?" she asks.

"Yes, I'll know. The sled team will bark. And so will the sheepdogs, and old Jorge is out there."

She continues, "Grandpa said that Coyote taught the sheep-dogs to herd sheep. And that every now and then Coyote Old Man takes one as payback."

She pauses,

"But Runner wants to shoot all the coyotes. Why?"

"He's afraid of losing all our sheep. And he wants the coyotes to be afraid. He doesn't really want to shoot ALL of the coyotes. Just wanted to scare them off, like Jorge the guard dog," I tell her.

"But how can God's sheepdog be Mike and Coyote Old Man and the Buddha's magic flower?"

I think for a moment,

"This is the problem when people tell so many different stories."

Finally I say,

"Well, maybe they appear different to different people. Maybe when people used a lot of plants, then flowers are God's special messengers. Maybe when they hunt and fish, the little clever coyote is their hero. And maybe when they raise sheep, God is a shepherd and he has Mike."

This seemed to satisfy the little girl.

"Auntie Tea? Will God take care of my Dad overseas in the war?"

My heart is breaking in that moment.

"Yes, honey, God will."

"Who should I ask to look out for him?"

Her eyes hold depth of feeling that as an adult I can scarcely carry now.

"Oh honey, ask all of them."

The sheepdogs twitch and dream.

The little girl climbs into my lap and we sit and the wind moans over the little cabin

And it's dark

And Pete is on the mainland.

§§§

The morning comes

The difference between night and day.

The dogs yawn and stretch

I find a letter my niece wrote to her Dad.

Dear Dad,

I am praying that you will be ok.

Be on the lookout for a big, black, slick-coated prick-eared sheepdog

He works for God.

I felt he was the best one to help watch over you. As I hear the war is being fought in lands that have one thing in common, all of them are sheep-herding folk.

Love Your Daughter,

Tsu

P. S. The dog's name is Mike.

American Lambs

My niece brought home a stray.

She found her walking home from school.

Stopped and the dog walked out of the grass.

Skinny little black bitch, with white-tipped toes and a soft brown-eyed gaze.

My niece remembered what her grandpa had told her.

She named her on the spot, Ta. (Deer)

And called the little dog that came slinking, tail wagging furiously, to her arms.

She begged to keep her.

What can I do?

My brother's only daughter and him long gone into the dust after the marines.

The little dog was a border collie, or sheepdog as my family called them.

About five years old.

My niece soon was begging me for lambs.

"Lambs! Aunt Tea, to train her."

"Ok, I give in. Here are four lambs.

Train your dog. Fatten these lambs and when we sell them I will give you a piece of the action."

She likes that phrase.

I see her out there,

She gets all the dog training videos. (Pete and her grand-mother . . .)

Pete wins a really thin TV at a raffle and the girl watches these videos all the time.

Poor Gunny, my dog, watches too, but thinks, "Why can't I get behind these sheep?" She is circling the thin TV.

I am always hearing

Come bye!
AWAY!!!
Wheeeeeeeeeeettttttt!!
That'll doooo, good lad . . . that'll doo good lad.

Some Scottish guy talking.

My niece begins to sound like the Scottish guy which con-fuses her cousins.

She asks me,

"Are we part Scottish?"

"Well, maybe a bit, married into the Native side. Adopted the Japanese side."

She wants to wear a kilt to school.

She works the little black bitch.

The little dog is pretty good.

At least in my opinion.

Six months pass by

Soon she begs

"Let's go to a dog trial . . . a dog trial! A sheep dog trial."

I tell her, "I don't have extra money, girl, to spend. I'm sorry.

I don't have time to go . . . I got to work.

Sell your lambs if you want and we will go."

Girl goes down to the fancy restaurant, the proprietor is Tlingit.

"Buy my lambs! Please."

She tells the restaurant that they are extraordinary hand-browsed lambs

Has the lambs done by the fancy new mobile USDA slaughterer

Brain tans the hides, sells them.

Girl makes more money per lamb than I do.

Saves her money.

Finds a trial . . . "Let's go Auntie Tea! Let's go."

"No, no, I am scared of those competition things, makes you crazy!"

"But that's just you, Aunt, not me, let's go, let's go!"

Between that and the thin TV spewing out

Come bye
Away
wheeeeeet wheeeettt,
that'll doooo, good lad
that'll dooooo good lad!

I cave.

We go to the trial.

§§§

"Do you know how to do this?"

I ask the girl.

Fifteen years old, she gives me that look.

"Of course, Auntie!"

Grandpa asks, "Why are there gates with no fences in the fields?"

"So it's harder," she answers.

Grandpa says, "Oh."

I tell him, "It gives you a lot of room to maneuver."

"Oh Auntie," my niece answers, "You have to go through them! And stay straight."

"I know, believe it or not Pete and I have watched one other dog trial. When is it your turn?"

"Soon! I'm going to go watch."

"Ok."

"Here, Grandpa, hold Ta."

She hands him a leash made of binder twine, braided.

The trial dog crowd is a mixed bag.

Some old farm trucks, some new fancy,

Some really fancy-looking dogs.

Some as slinky as coyotes.

I look at the sheep.

Fast, yearling ewes, like antelopes.

Hum, I figure hanging weight in my head.

Grandpa says, "Are those really sheep? They must be foreign sheep! They have really short wool, and they don't look like they've been sheared."

"Grandpa, they're bred to have no wool." I tell him.

Grandpa raises his eyebrows, rather startled, like the lambs were from the moon.

My niece walks back, whispers to her grandpa not to be sheep prejudiced. Then she walks off again.

People are friendly.

The organizer comes and talks to us and soon we have it figured out, or so we think.

A woman comes up to Grandpa and says, "That's a nice dog, she looks familiar. What else do you do with her?"

Pete and I turn to watch this unfold, better than the thin TV.

Grandpa squints up his eyes; "Oh, I'm thinking of hunting her after rabbits this fall. She'd be a top-notch rabbit dog."

"Oh?" the lady says carefully, "Well, who do you train with, where do you take her to work sheep?"

Grandpa thinks a moment, "Oh, well now, we have sheep at home."

He adds so there is no confusion,

"But AMERICAN sheep, proper island sheep."

Grandpa then says with a slight Scottish accent, "Come bye, Away! That'll dooo . . . good lad!"

Grandpa had been watching the thin TV.

Of course we know he is teasing, but Grandpa Humor can be difficult to grasp.

The lady smiles a little confused smile and walks away. (Almost backs away.)

Soon my niece comes back, and notices this scene.

"Try not to talk to too many people, ok?" She says to her family.

She is excited her turn is next.

My niece takes Ta and kneels down and strokes her face.

"Do good, Ta!" she tells her.

They go proudly to the handler's post

And wait a moment.

The sheep are far away at the top of a green crowned hill.

She sends the dog out

Little Ta runs out wide enough

Gets behind her sheep

And gently brings them down straight as a promise towards our girl.

At one moment out of sight behind the rise of the land.

But my girl waits for heaven and soon Ta appears with the sheep in front of her as quiet as mice.

My niece's face shines like the sunlight.

The little dog's white-tipped toes flash in the grass

Around the girl, they swing the whole lot. Like constellations around the North Star.

They cross the field and trot through gates, swing around.

The girl has whistled maybe three or four times.

And a few quiet words to the dog when they were close.

Finally

She steps away to pen

The sheep are reluctant, one stomping big ewe lamb in particular.

The ewes finally make it into the pen

And my little girl shuts the gate

Triumph sparks from her eyes.

People clap! Bless them.

She comes back

And we all sit on the tailgate of our truck to have lunch.

Which the farm cooks and sells reasonably.

Ta is looking at a truck.

My niece notices this.

An older man with a cowboy hat is watching Ta, and Ta is watching him.

She is wagging her tail.

My niece turns and looks into my eyes.

Heartbreak, knowledge, adulthood.

Grandpa puts his hand on her shoulder.

"Little girl, Ta wants to go to that man," he tells her.

"Let her go and see what she does."

My niece slips off the binder twine leash and Ta gives a quick glance up at her and then runs in great leaps to the man and jumps up so high she touches his cheek.

He kneels down and strokes her, his face and expression mercifully hidden.

He soon stands and walks over to us, Ta behind his right leg as if glued there.

He offers his hand to my niece

She shakes it, lightly grasping only his two fingers.

"Honey, this is my dog I lost last year, my Open-level dog."

My niece swallows. "I know, I can see she's yours."

The man says slowly, softly,

"You saved her, I think. She was lost and you found her and cared for her. Is that what happened? That deserves a reward.

I'll give you a pup from her . . . I know you love her. I can see that. But will that be all right?"

Grandpa nods at my niece

She sighs

"Yes." Then touches Ta on the top of her head.

My niece got ninth at her first sheepdog trial

And something happened, more importantly, that taught her to become

A good person

Because of a lost dog,

A Scottish guy and a thin TV,

A dog trial,

And a kind stranger.

Foreign lambs

And four American ones.

§§§

That'll dooo, good lad! That'll doooo . . . Good lad.

Grippy

My old pop died young. But before he died when I was a girl, he told me this story. I am writing this down for you Tsu, so you understand where part of your family came from, the part that is not talked about too much.

Pop was born in a village in Sicily. His family emigrated to America when he was about seven years old, his mother and father and his six brothers and two younger sisters. Pop was the quiet one, who loved animals.

They landed first in Hell's Kitchen, Pop called it. He never told me where that was, but it is somewhere in New York City and I guess it is a wild place.

Kind of like the Elk Horn Bar east of the rez in Montana, where your second cousin Bobby gets into all those fights because he thinks cowboys are staring at him.

Pop's family were in the liquor business. They transported alcohol from one spot to another for folks to sell. I guess New York wasn't paying too much attention to the fact that it was Prohibition.

Anyway, your great grandmother, Pop's mom, decided the family had to move out into the country to get away from the heat. I guess it gets pretty hot back east. Turns out Great Grandpa was good at making wine but he kept throwing the grape skins out the window and somebody got wise. The family looked for a house with land where they could keep goats and sheep. Finally they found a nice house that Great Grandma loved. It was on Long Island. It had some land where she could keep sheep and goats.

It was for sale. Then the guy that owned it decided not to sell it when he met the family. I guess he didn't like immigrants.

Well Great Grandma complained to her husband, your great grandfather, and he complained to Jimmy. Now Jimmy was your grandpa's nephew on his elder sister's side. He had been born in Sicily but moved to America many years earlier and he was a Made Man. You'll have to look that one up; I'm not sure what this exactly means.

Jimmy had wild curly black hair like a lamb. He was a very handsome guy and a lot of young ladies were dying of love for him. He was called Jimmy Marino. He was a gentleman and called upon Great Grandma and Grandpa for advice regarding red sauce or who he should marry. Sauce is a big thing to that side of the family. So is who you marry, but sauce may be more important.

Jimmy was fond of the old folks. So when Great Grandpa told him what had happened about the house for sale on Long Island, Jimmy Marino hugged him and told him that he would take care of it.

Well the guy that owned that house disappeared. No one ever saw him again. So the whole family moved right in. And Grandma got her goats and sheep. They also had one hog.

Anyway, Pop's job was to take care of the sheep and milk the goats. He loved animals. Pop was soft-hearted and often got teased for dreaming and writing poetry.

Well one day Pop was bringing the sheep up the road. I guess he took them to the neighbors to get sheared. And he saw a guy beating a dog. And I mean beating. The dog curled up on its back and this guy whaling on him with his belt. Buckle end.

Pop ran over and tried to stop this man. But the guy then turned his attention on Pop and started beating him as well, a few licks for Pop then back to beating the dog. Then the guy kicked Pop for a bit, and then kicked the dog. All the time Pop hoping that the dog would run or the guy would get tired, Pop tried to shield the dog with his body, he bit the guy on the leg. I mean it was a battle.

Well as it turns out the shearing guy was an Irishman who liked whiskey and he bought it from our family.

All this dust was causing some commotion and who should come out of the shearing guy's house but Jimmy Marino. He runs up with his two friends and freaks completely out. Pop said he was screaming in Sicilian at this dog-beating guy and pulls out a gun and then Jimmy and his friends grab The Dog Beater and throw him into the trunk of their car.

Then Jimmy goes back and helps Pop up out of the dirt, and looks him over. The dog gets up too. You guessed it, a little tri-colored sheepdog. Pop isn't crying, he is trying to be brave, he was about ten. He remembers Jimmy's eyes. He said he looked crazy. Like a mad man. Jimmy then tells Pop to go home and take the poor dog. Then he jumps into his car with his buddies and they drive off with the dog-beating guy in the trunk screaming and hollering.

The Irishman shearer guy watches them drive off and crosses himself and says about fifty Hail Mary's.

Pop goes home. Great Grandma nearly has a heart attack at the sight of him. But anyway to make a longer story shorter, Pop healed and so did this little dog. Now Pop had a helper to move sheep and goats.

This dog was named by Jimmy. His name was Capo.

Well it turns out that this dog was a pretty good sheepdog. And the Irish shearer taught Pop how to work him. The family thought the world of this dog as they had never seen anything like him before.

The dog and Pop were good friends. And this little dog would hunt rabbits as well.

One day Pop takes him to deliver pecorino cheese to a little restaurant that had opened up near Woodmere.

A cop stops him outside and wants to see the dog license for Pop's dog. Capo did not have a license. But who steps out of the restaurant but Jimmy Marino.

The cop then says that Capo is such a good dog he will never have to have a dog license, ever.

Jimmy tells him, "Thanks, it's like Capo has an invisible dog license that lasts forever."

Jimmy pats the cop on the back and invites him inside for a drink. Pop goes home with his dog.

Then one day the dog catcher grabs Capo on the road and takes him to the dog pound. In those days dogs got gassed at the dog pound if they didn't have a license. And the dog catcher didn't know that Capo had a lifetime invisible license.

Pop went nuts trying to find his dog. The Irish shearer and Pop go down to the dog pound and there is Capo. But the dog catcher won't give him back. They plead with him, beg him. But he says, "Nope, I'm gassing him, he doesn't have a license."

Pop tells him, "Capo has a lifetime license, but it's invisible."

The dog catcher laughs. And says, "Forget about it, kid."

The Irish Shearer tells Pop to stay there and keep the dog catcher talking. The Irishman runs two miles to Betty Soriano's house who Jimmy Marino was courting. Luck would have it that Jimmy was there with his guys. By the way, Betty was a great beauty. Jimmy always got the best girls.

He tells Jimmy the predicament Capo is in. Jimmy and his friends and the Irish Shearer jump into the car and drive down to the dog pound. They make the shearer and Pop wait outside. Soon they come out with Capo. They look a bit out of breath.

Jimmy straightens his tie and laughs, and he tells Pop, "Bambino, you and your dog sure get into a lot of trouble."

Pop goes home.

That next day Pop is out hunting rabbits with Capo and they meet Jimmy and some of his friends. They are digging a hole in the deep woods. Pop told me that they said they were looking for truffles. But Pop knew that could not be true, because they would have brought Grandma's hog.

As for Capo he lived to extreme old age. And he never was without his invisible dog license and nobody ever bothered him. In fact people were always giving him treats, especially if Jimmy was around.

Everydog
(For Arnuk and Gunny)

I am afraid

It is cold in here

I hear other dogs

They are warning

They are angry

They are afraid

They are sad

Voices

Calling people

I am here?

Where are you?

This moment is forever for me

I was a puppy once

I was a young dog once.

I was an old dog.

I was a sick dog.

I worked for a living.

I comforted as a job.

I played to create joy.

I am Everydog.

But now I am here.

Where is here?

Where are you?

Are you coming?

I feel your hands on my ears.

I see your face in my dreams.

I slept near you at night.

Are you coming for me?

Someone comes.

They take me out into the sunshine.

And there you are.

I come to you and breathe in your scent.

With you now

All is forgotten.

I am home being near you.

This moment is forever to me.

We walk away to the old truck I know so well.

I get in.

As we drive off

I hear dogs barking.

Hay for Sale

The hay is stacked in three piles.

Bedding.

All right.

And really good.

Bedding is the color of late summer.

All right is the color of late spring.

And really good is a sweet green and smells like childhood days spent outside.

It is stacked on pallets that are donated by the grocery store.

Hastily nailed together, but they keep the hay off the ground, where earth reaches up with unseen, dark hands and pulls it back down to herself.

She only lets us keep it temporarily.

The hay is stacked between tall fir trees and tarped with reluctant plastic that flaps and cracks when the spooked flock trots by, making my dogs earn their keep.

There is an old chair by the hay pile with a mason jar perched on it. The lid is hard to remove.

Inside is a note.

It reads

Hay for Sale

Bedding: $3.00
All Right: $5.00
Really good: $20

Please leave money in jar. Put lid on, ravens will take money out of jar, and they refuse to pay the bills.

Gunny at the Grocery Store

Gunny ever patient waits for me outside the store and meets various dogs coming up to the doorway or passing by.

These are their conversations:

Black dog with red bandana

"What are you doing?"

"Quiet, numbskull, I'm watching these gates."

"Why are you watching them?"

"That should be apparent. Go find a duck."

The black dog wanders away

A woman and a pug dog walk up. The woman stops to read the bulletin board.

"Hello," the pug says to Gunny, cheerfully, "I am very beautiful. This is my friend. Isn't she lovely? What a great day it is. Don't you think?"

Gunny gives the dog a quick withering glance.

"Oh, good God!"

The woman and the pug walk away. The pug giving the dog equivalent of shrugging its shoulders.

A man comes out of the store and looks down.

Oh poor doggy? You lost?

Gunny never taking her eyes off the door, side passes his hands that reach down to pat her.

He reaches down once more, concern in his expression. Gunny fixes him with her caramel-eyed glare reserved for tough cows and he whips his hands back up and mutters, "Well, you're most likely waiting for somebody."

Another man walks up and ties his young dog to the dog ring that was installed in the wall. This pup is a border collie.

His owner goes into the hardware store next door.

The pup notices right away that Gunny is intently watching the doors.

He starts watching them too.

"What's going to happen?" he whispers in a serious way.

"Tea just went in there. She is probably opening gates inside; then I'll go in and move the sheep back out towards our rig over there."

"Oh? Well, can I help you? I would be glad to."

"I suppose. But keep sharp now. I think it's ewes with young lambs."

Pioneers

It's not about money

That's the mistake.

Money is only paper.

It is about cold mornings and frying lamb chops.

It's about stomping snow as you walk with joy down to stock that are glad to see you.

I watch the sheep browse and I don't see money.

I see peace.

I see self-sufficiency.

It's about yogurt and real milk.

About cheese that melts like new cream in your mouth.

Real food.

It's about pulling on socks that last longer than a month and are warmer than summertime.

Real clothes.

I go to sleep next to Pete and dream of grass and sounds of hooves.

I look at my dogs as partners in our lives.

When I sell things at the market

I tell people,

"I will teach you how."

Some want to learn.

Others only want to buy.

Missing the real gifts.

I almost resent selling them real things.

Because the money is just paper

And it seems a poor trade.

Sheep in Space

On Bush Island it can get a bit boring. That's why around April Fools Day we started doing a few jokes. They got very elaborate.

Pete and my brothers and I saw a documentary about crop circles on TV. We decided that the week before April Fools Day we would have UFOs land on the Island.

As the population of our island changed, a lot of folks that moved here believed in all kinds of interesting things and UFOs were one of them. Why they thought UFOs would visit such a backwater as Bush Island I do not know. Most visitors go to Seattle or Victoria BC.

The night of our big caper we got all our gear together. We needed a length of rope and some boards to make our circles. Grandpa told us to wear our moccasins so we wouldn't leave any tracks.

We went to this hill in the center of the Island. The sheep hadn't been in there, yet. And the grass was long and soft.

We created our UFO landing area by having someone stand in the middle of our circle with a rope. The rope was attached to our board and we gently pushed the board around in a circle and carefully bent the grasses down. The trick is to bend the grasses, not break them. That is very important in UFO-style crop circles.

We stood back admiring the circles. Then my brother—your father, Tsu, got a great idea.

We would light up the sheep. We went back and got our sheepdog Cap and gathered up about twenty old ewes and one horned ram. Then we stuck reflectors on them. These little reflectors had backs that you peeled the paper off and they were sticky. We got them from the Harbor store. This delighted the owner as we bought about all she had.

One by one we caught the ewes and put these things all over them. On the ram we only stuck them to his horns.

The idea was that he was the Captain.

Then we turned the sheep loose around our crop circle.

You see these fields were situated on the bend of the main road. You are driving out in the middle of nowhere on this dark island and you come around the corner and your head-lights hit these reflectors and then the whole thing looks like a twirling glittering light show, especially if Cap is moving the sheep around.

So we lay in the bushes and I whistle at Cap as the first car approaches. The headlights hit the sheep and the show is on. Sheep swirl and move and glitter and the car slams on its breaks. There is a moment of silence and I down Cap.

The sheep stop moving.

The car whips around and takes off the other way! We laugh so hard we are crying!

We do this again and again to perhaps five or six cars. Finally we have Cap re-gather the sheep and take the reflectors off.

Then we leave.

That next week when I get the island paper I notice a big article about lights near Quartermaster fields.

It has a picture of our crop circle. I hear on the radio that afternoon that some UFO experts are flying in to examine it. Airplanes begin circling the fields.

One guy tells the newspaper that the UFO made the sheep radioactive. This is later disproved by the UFO experts with a Geiger counter. However the UFO guys swear that some alien substance was detected on the sheep. Now this might have been glue from the reflectors or stuff for lice. But anyway UFOs were thought to have left it on the sheep.

We got a kick out of all of this. For a year there were weekly UFO meetings at the grange hall. People wanted to be sure they knew what to do when the UFOs landed.

Years later when Pete and I were having dinner at the Quartermaster Pub, some folks from Hollywood came in and sat down with the tug boat captain, Captain John. Captain John was telling them about the landing at Quartermaster fields and how it was never explained. These guys from Hollywood were making a movie about UFOs.

They sat and talked and had dinner at the pub, which, by the way, served our lamb.

We listened gravely till Captain John told them why the lamb from Bush Island was so good.

"It's the sheep," he said. "Some of our sheep are from space."

The Professionals

The old dog lay panting, watching ten sheep graze the dry grass. The sheep kept one eye on him, especially the collared lead ewe.

An old man, sitting bent on a blue roan gelding, watched quietly as another dog came up the hill. That dog was running low and smooth and fast and circled around the back of the flock.

The old dog and the rider on the roan stood still as the new dog took control of the ewes.

The other dog lifted the sheep and set off with them down the hill towards the post and the crowd of spectators. It was the beginning of a spectacular run and the crowd was quiet.

The old dog got up slowly and, limping, followed the horseman back towards the set-out gate.

As he did, he started up a conversation with the blue roan gelding.

"Mind where you step, Partner."

"Sorry, flies are bad. What do you suppose the two legs are up to?" The horse asked the dog. He was a four-year-old off the range and had only been started under saddle this last spring.

The dog, a rough-coated tri-colored beast, paused and looked back down the hill where the crossdrive was beginning.

"It's a kind of practice."

The horse shook his head which made the reins flap.

"Practice for what?"

The dog then did stop and looked up at the horse.

"Why, practice for range work of course. The dogs come here and practice till they are real good, then they go off and work."

"I see," said the horse. "Well then, did you do this sort of thing?"

The old dog replied, "Nope, never did. But I watched my mother a lot when I was young, so maybe I didn't need much practice."

The rider and dog began to move another small group of sheep out toward the set out. The sheep were stubborn Dorsets but they floated in front of the dog like dandelion fluff. No challenge did they present.

The rider stopped the blue roan gelding and the dog allowed the sheep to drift a bit. Then the dog circled a quarter ways around them and lay down. Never a word was spoken by the old man.

"What will we do tomorrow do you think?" asked the horse.

"Move sheep," the dog stated firmly.

"And the day after that?"

"Move more sheep. That is what we do. It is a very important thing. That's why my old man is up before dawn and feeds when the snow is deep. See, he is thin and ancient now, worn out in the service of this great task of sheep."

Another dog was running wide up the hill to lift the flock. The old dog moved closer to the old horseman.

The Dorsets turned to the young dog as he approached and the lead ewe told him. "You have got to be kidding me, get lost."

The sheep returned to grazing.

The young dog hearing his master's frantic whistle was desperate.

"My partner is so far away . . ." He complained to the old dog who was watching him, not moving, from a safe distance.

"Get down and walk up real slow, like a cat after a bird. Put a wolf in your eyes . . . and mean it . . . go on now, you can do it," the old dog says to the young dog.

The blue roan cocked one hind leg. The roan heard the old man chuckle. The roan wondered if he could understand their conversations. The old man stroked his neck.

The young dog took a deep breath and slunk up softly towards the sheep who slowly changed their opinion of him and moved off.

"Greenhorn," the old dog told the roan.

The roan said, "That is good of you to help him. After all, he's not even a relation."

"I know, but someone has to help these young guys. And I guess it's us. But it can only be a comment or two. I can't move his sheep for him; it's against my old man's beliefs. Oh, here comes Jill and Lucy dog."

A woman jogged up on a sorrel mare with a black freckled bitch.

The two people spoke briefly.

The old man on the roan turned away.

"Come on Ted, lunch for us, old timer," he told his dog.

The dog walked away after the roan and soon was lying next to a dented Ford truck, drinking some water out of a soup pot with a broken handle. The roan, bridle off, halter on and girth loose, stood flicking flies. The old man was eating a hot dog, and sipping a soda pop. He had spilled some on his best shirt, carefully ironed by his wife years ago and laid in a drawer. He brushed at it with a paper napkin.

A young man and a young dog walked up, and the young man reached for the old man's calloused hand before he could stand up from his yellow folding lawn chair.

"Well, hi there," the old man said as he put down his pop and shuffled his hot dog to his left hand.

The young man smiled, "Hey, thanks so much for helping today. We sure needed help for the trial. There were only a few volunteers this year."

"Not a problem, young man. I watched your dog; he did well. These ewes were stubborn."

"They were. I was worried at the lift. You saw how slow everything happened. But then Lad really changed, he got down and went to work like a pro."

The old man smiled and bent down and ruffled Ted's ears.

"Yep, like a pro."

Ettrick Shepherding

I watched the sky and saw an eagle high over my head. Mary's voice brought me back to reality as my "good dog," Gunny, scattered her flock of sheep like a bomb had burst through them. She ran nipping, smiling the whole while. I yelled at her to stop.

Finally she did stop and turned and gave me a look that told me she thought this was really fun.

My poor friend told me cheerfully, "You know, she can't do that, she's running pounds off these sheep."

"Yes. That is very true." I answered.

This was Gunny's first time in a big pasture. I browse my sheep loose on the forest trails at my place, but wanting to continue learning I decided to seek out help from my friend Mary. I piled all my dogs into Grandpa's pickup and drove over to her farm.

Mary trials and is a cheerful and patient instructor.

After the initial bust up of sheep, we took Gunny to a smaller pen with some dog-broke sheep. Mary instructed me on the finer points of sheepdog work.

I discovered something that day. I daydream constantly.

The sheep were very willing to follow me around in the smaller paddock.

But I begin thinking of poetry. Sadly, thinking of poetry interferes with working sheep. The sheep followed me and Gunny crowded them and the sheep started to push past me, which brought me back from poetry to the fact that Mary was telling me something.

Mary told me patiently, "Uh . . . Tea . . . you're walking in a circle, you need to back up in a straight line." I started backing up.

It was a very sweet afternoon in early February, clear cold skies, with just a hint that spring was not far away. I looked up into a fir tree where a small cooper's hawk was sitting on a broken branch. They are shy accipiters, true forest hawks. A poem about hawks began forming in my head.

Mary's voice interrupted, "Uh, Tea, you have to quit saying 'Gunny Gunny' all the time, I don't think the dog knows what you're talking about, and now she's just sitting there."

I looked at Gunny. She was just sitting there looking at me with a funny look on her face.

Ok, forget poetry, forget hawks. Try to concentrate. I began backing up and backed into the fence, then backed into some tree branches . . . The sheep, hum . . . the wool . . . I reached out to feel the closest sheep's face . . . Nice wool for spinning.

"Uh . . . Tea, flank the dog . . . flank the dog . . ."

"Oh, yeah . . ."

Finally we stopped and I watched Mary work her dogs.

They went out, gathered sheep, stopped, did everything beautifully. And I could tell Mary could really concentrate. I formed a few more poems while I watched them work.

"Sheepdog moves lambs like wind moves trees

Like water moving leaves

Soft ripples on the face of a slow river

That sparkles and winks over rocks ancient and bright."

Then I realized that Mary was trying to explain things to me and I wasn't paying enough attention to understand what she had just said. I was trying to memorize my poem so that I could write it down when I got home. I felt it would be impolite to stop and ask for paper and pen.

We decided to get out Sweep the Broom and worked him for a bit. He did better than me. I kept thinking of things that compared to his black fur and fierce trembling energy.

Finally we finished and I put my dogs back into Grandpa's truck.

Then Mary and I sat down and shot the breeze for awhile.

Mary told me, "It'll help you in the long run."

I looked at my dogs sitting in the truck, staring at the sheep in Mary's pasture.

Then far away I heard the clear voice of a courting eagle, a shrill musical chirruping. The eagle so high in the evening sky I could not see him.

"Yes," I told Mary. Another poem floated lazily into my head.

Softly, like a message from another world, I heard Mary sigh.

Kippy

————————————————————————————————————

Before my niece had found Ta, when she was about twelve years old, she got the word from a friend at school that there was going to be a dog show on the Island.

Now realize when I say dog show, the mayor of our small town would judge it and how you would win would be any-one's guess. It was a country kind of thing set up to bring attention to the plight of homeless pets, in conjunction with our harvest fair.

Well the little girl came to me and asked if she could take a dog to this show and enter it in a class. I saw the National Velvet flag raise up in her eyes. This means a child sees themselves winning something over incredible odds with an animal, usually a dog or a horse.

I told her that right now I couldn't spare any of the working sheepdogs and the only available dog was Kippy.

Kippy was a huge furry malamute sled dog, one of my wheel dogs that could be trusted in public. His main job in life was to pull heavy objects. This he did with good humor and a calm manner.

His personality was like a great big grumpy tired old bear. And his fur was like he was preparing to go with Byrd to the South Pole.

Kippy growled all the time. He growled when you petted him, he growled to himself. He was not a dog that would bite, but he sure liked to growl a lot.

When Maria the mail lady delivered our mail, if Kippy was outside, she dropped the envelopes on the ground without getting out of her car.

When I told Tsu she could use Kippy it at first delighted her. Kippy had pulled her through the woods on the red sled as a little girl and she had a bond with him.

She started brushing him. Great mounds of hair came off which I actually spun to make a hat. We found Kippy hair on everything, in our food, in the sink, clinging to the windows.

One day while we were standing in line at the bank, the man next to me looked down at his sweater and started brushing at it. The teller met my eyes.

I looked down.

Kippy hair was floating off me and drafting towards the man, who couldn't figure out where this fur was coming from, and he shot a couple of startled glances towards the ceiling.

After Kip was cleaned up, then my niece wanted to take him to the retired school teacher that taught dog classes.

Grandpa and I took them, although we were not sure what was meant by dog classes. But my niece thought it was important.

Kippy being a sled dog knew all of his commands to work the sled, in fact he could have run lead but he didn't really have the motivation so that was left to more inspired dogs.

We arrived at the lady's house for dog class. There were other kids and some adults there with dogs. Grandpa was amazed by the size and shape of so many different dogs. In fact some he didn't believe to be dogs at all.

He kept saying, "My God, look at THAT one!"

Till my niece asked him to please not freak people out.

Kippy had walked in at the end of his binder twine braided leash, growling the whole time. He sat down and then as soon as the teacher started talking about aspects of positive dog training, he gave a warning gag then promptly threw up.

My niece shot a look of utter horror and pleading in my direction and I came forward and Grandpa ran to get a towel from the truck. The teacher was very kind and said not to be bothered as it must have been something he had eaten.

Of course as the smell spread it was easy to understand that whatever he had eaten had been dead long before Kippy had consumed it.

Grandpa announced it was a chipmunk. And sadly held up the remains to show the class that he was correct.

One student backed away from the scene as fast as she could pull her dog, who was unfortunately trying to inspect the remains of Kippy's meal. Kippy was growling at the dog.

We went to the class every week. It became an ordeal.

I worried about my niece as she sweated and pulled that big dog through his paces.

Kippy seemed doomed to do everything he possibly could to embarrass her.

Kippy peed on another dog, marking it as property. It was a small poodlish dog and the owner was frantic, wiping the dog with my purse which she had grabbed out of my hands.

He growled every time the teacher took his leash so that she finally stayed away from the pair.

He had diarrhea all over the floor after consuming some other unmentionable thing.

Then one day he got amorous with a flat-coated retriever. Sadly it was a male who didn't appreciate a big furry dog climbing on him and the fight that ensued could be heard from the next farm over, which sent people running thinking perhaps that a bear had gotten inside the house.

The flat-coated retriever wisely took refuge under the teacher who was knocked to the ground.

Grandpa grabbed Kip by the hind legs and pulled him off the other dog. No one was hurt. But Kippy and Tsu were now told to stand at the back of the class.

Where Kippy wore a smile on his northern dog face.

The young man with the border collie gave my niece his most understanding gaze. He and his dog were at the front of the class, often showing how to execute the maneuvers.

The commands were hard for Kippy, heel and sit and lie down and stay. Kippy sometimes looked at Tsu with genuine confusion in his brown old eyes.

He could make nothing out of it, I could tell. It became a pushing match. And Kippy was winning.

So pretty much the dog class was failing.

But my niece did not give up. Like Velvet Brown she saw herself winning this dog show, against incredible odds.

I know my niece sighed and pined that all our sheepdogs were working. She thought in her heart that our sheepdogs could do this class with ease and win the dog show hands down.

And she was stuck with Kippy.

The boy with the border collie was sympathetic to her and patted Kippy even when he growled. The boy told her he was a fabulous dog.

We took Kippy to my friend who had the only dog grooming establishment on the Island. Kippy was promptly banned from that place. She called me on the phone minutes after I had left to say that she couldn't put Kippy in a kennel or get him to do anything. Kippy had in fact taken over the office and was in there now growling at nothing at all.

When Grandpa and I came to get him, she had put his photo up on the wall of BANNED DOGS. (Everyone on the Island knows your dogs.)

Grandpa became fascinated with the dog grooming equipment and said he could get Kippy properly trimmed. He did it by hand with sheep blades.

This became an adventure for Kippy who lost most of his coat and looked like a big lamb slick sheared for state fair.

My niece asked me if he looked funny. I scratched my chin and looked at the big dog standing there wagging his tail.

"Well, it'll grow back a bit before the show."

Finally the day of the dog show arrived and we stood on the commons grass and waited for the judge to tell the contestants what to do.

It was to be a course without a leash. A walk around obstacles, orange road cones. Then, lie down, and then turn right and walk, then a left turn and stay. The obstacle thought the most difficult was the walk by a raw lamb chop strategically placed on the ground on a plate with silver chickens parading around the rim.

Some contestants had thought the raw lamb chop dangerous for dogs to eat, in case a dog accidentally snapped it up. But Grandpa bent down and cut off a sliver with his pocket knife and popped it into his mouth, then proclaimed it safe enough for dogs.

Tsu put her face in her hands.

My poor niece was sad. Her National Velvet Dreams were slipping away like Kippy's shed fur.

Dogs and their owners one at a time started the course. One yappy little dog knocked down all the cones. One lab ran away presumably to go home.

One other big dog just lay down and refused to move.

The border collie and the young man did extremely well, only one cone got knocked down as they walked around the course. Several others did as good with only minor mistakes.

Tsu and Kippy were last.

Just before it was Tsu's turn. I became inspired. I came up to Tsu and whispered, "Tsu, use Kippy's sled dog commands. Gee and haw and whoa and line out . . . you know them all. Use those commands, like you were using the toboggan sled and pulling firewood."

Tsu's obsidian eyes gleamed and she nodded her head vigorously.

Then it was her turn.

She told the big dog, "Ok . . ."

He walked with her smoothly.

"Now, Gee." The dog turned right with her.

"Haw, Kip!"

The dog turned left with her.

"Whoa!" Kippy stopped.

"Wait!" said the girl; Kippy lay down and watched her.

"Whoa, Kip," she said again and my niece walked away.

The crowd was hushed; everyone had thought that our Kippy was going to be the amusing part of the show.

Kippy lay there and watched.

Even the border collie watched.

Then Tsu went to the big dog and proceeded to walk him past the lamb chop, gleaming on its plate with silver chickens dancing enticingly around the rim.

"ON BY!" She told him sternly. Kip didn't even glance at it.

And that is how our wheel dog won our local dog show. The only dog show anyone in the family had ever entered.

But insidiously it began developing the National Velvet Idea in my niece's head that came to its highest point the day she found Ta.

The Last Trail

———————————————————————————————

That morning Grandpa had gotten up before all the rest of us. He had made coffee, because when I got up it was simmering on the woodstove.

Then he pulled on his boots and stumped down to the barn. One old dog went with him. The ewes had one-month-old lambs at their side. Grandpa sent in the dog, opened the leaning gate and took the sheep out towards the highest meadow we use, beyond the logging trails and the cathedral of trees.

He walked slowly. I could tell by his tracks. It was a sweet young morning in April. It had rained that night, but the grass was coming up quick and immortal in its bright green.

Grandpa sat leaning against a fir tree overlooking the little meadow when I found him. Old Dog lay quiet nearby. The ewes were grazing in the morning light. And the light flickered and danced on the mountain's glaciers in the distance.

He was by a house that had been foreclosed. No one had lived here for a long time. I knelt by Grandpa for a moment, my warm hand on his cold one. I wondered if children would play here in the long grass and peer into the deep woods. And maybe they would sense the presence of our dogs and sheep, and a dear old man.

Grandpa's eyes were open, even in death he still watched the sheep.

I got out my cell phone and called the family. Tsu answered the phone.

"Grandpa has gone now, Tsu."

Tsu choked back a quiet sob. "Oh, Auntie . . ."

"He is very peaceful, little girl, sitting in the high meadow, by the old foreclosed house. Tell your uncle. I will wait here."

Tsu told me, the young comforting the old, "Remember the grass, Auntie, how it comes up every spring in the circle dance."

I laughed a dry choke of a laugh and added, "Remember Mike the Sheepdog of God, little Tsu, because Grandpa is striding heaven with him and helping watch the flocks of the Good Shepherd."

I hung up, then glanced around the meadow following Grandpa's still gaze.

All around us the lambs ran and played, in long bright grass in sunlight sharp and warm.

The Story of Ta Two

I saw it in her eyes.

The whole thing.

I saw the screech of truck tires and wild scramble of hooves as sheep fled in all directions

The thump.

And this instant of longing for immortal things when your eyes watch with helpless desperation how mortal and fragile all life is.

Especially for a dog.

§§§

The pup was named Ta Two after Ta, the wanderer, who Tsu found one day marching through thick wild island grass.

Ta Two was a black bitch with a slick coat and ears that tilted down at the tips. She had white toes and kind eyes.

As I grew older Tsu took over the sheep browsing, and Ta Two helped her.

Of course there were roads to cross.

The pup grew up.

Became a fine working dog.

But life is life.

§§§

We took Ta Two to the vet that day.

We rushed here and there for the money to save her life.

All the Islanders contributed to help her.

But really they were helping Tsu.

Because deep down everyone wished that when they themselves had lost something as precious as a first dog that a miracle would present itself.

And sometimes miracles appear, like lambs in long grass that spring up as you walk through the fields.

Ta came home from her ordeal.

She was brave and showed that the courage of a dog

Shames humanity.

Tsu tended her day and night

And reminded us of the belief of youth,

(My Little Velvet Brown)

We gave Ta a ceremony to honor her commitment to her sheep

As she was run over in the line of duty.

Eventually she recovered to run another day.

§§§

Tsu grew up.

Went off to ride horses and see the world.

Ta grew old with us

And the sheep she loved.

Till one day she trailed herself to Grandpa's resting spot.

(She had never known him.)

And there she lay down and gave herself up, politely, to creation.

Tsu came home and was silent when I told her.

But I saw Ta's life flash gloriously in her eyes.

Power

⎯⎯⎯⎯⎯⎯⎯⎯⎯⎯⎯⎯⎯⎯⎯⎯⎯⎯⎯⎯⎯⎯⎯⎯

The fact is the goats had jumped out of the corral like so many gazelles and my little brown dog turned back to look at me as if to say, "Sorry, but nobody better try to butt me again."

Julie was sitting in her wheelchair and her breath was making smoky rings in the cold air. It was unusually cold, down to about ten degrees.

These goats had been a winter windfall for Julie who had just recently sold them. I had almost not brought my dog as I knew Julie had a dog.

We had backed the stock truck up to the corral and lowered the ramp, put some hay in and a sprinkling of grain.

I say to Julie's daughter, a sprite of a girl, "Send your dog up to fetch them."

I noticed that the dog, a young black-and-white boy, with sweet eyes, had looked despondent when he saw the stock truck. And now he was creeping away to hide behind the stacks of unsplit firewood rounds.

"Oh my dog won't get them," the girl told me.

"Why ever not?" I reply.

"Those does are killers. They chase him all over the fields. He is scared of them."

"Oh."

So I sent out Gunny.

Gunny the quick marine, no diplomacy, make peace or die as they say in the Corps.

The does formed a wall facing her and Gunny slowed and marched up to them. I only used her name.

My way of telling her I was here but she might need to make her own decisions on how to go about her work.

"Gun Gun. Gun Gun . . ."

One doe reared up on her hind legs, turned her head, and, horns down, decided to teach this upstart dog a lesson.

Gunny met her halfway and I think the doe had her eyes closed because her expression was incredulous when she opened them. Gunny nipped her and was back down on solid ground looking her in the eye.

The doe decided this must have been some kind of trick and tried it one more time.

Gunny saw it coming and again leaped up, got the feel of goat lips, and let go.

The does then decided this was an impossible reality and took off towards the far end of the corral.

"Gunny, come bye," I sang out to her.

Gunny circled around behind and the does stopped and began backing towards the stock trailer.

They backed up to the ramp and the whole group came to a dead halt.

"Gunny, hold there."

Gunny was smiling. So were the goats.

The does decided to take off at that moment and split up and ran off leaving Gunny and me a bit taken aback.

When they came to the short gate they were over it quick. They were yearling does and open. They jumped like their ancestors roamed the Serengeti.

It took us another thirty minutes to round them all up and finally load the darn things.

Then lift Julie into the truck. Julie was a quadriplegic.

She was an old friend. Her husband had left her with two young daughters, a rundown farm of toggenburg dairy goats and a lot of bills. She had called me to come out and drive the goats to the farmer who had bought them. I said I would. Julie then told me that she needed to talk to me.

She was a tough person. After being in the car accident she had lived with almost unbelievable pain and suffering in the hospital. But now she was home, and she had sold some goats. She wanted me to drive them, and she wanted to talk to me.

The truck was an old, big, flatbed Ford with handmade wooden sides. A stick shift . . . dusty, brakes squishy, old tires with worn studs.

We set out.

"It isn't far." Julie said.

We drive across a winter landscape of tall firs draped with thick snow and the quiet that is wintertime. Occasionally we pass a house with a friendly fire putting out wood smoke, blue and thin into the air.

Julie was silent the whole way. She sat crouched and bent in the passenger seat staring out the window, her breath fogging the glass that she couldn't wipe away. The countryside was hidden by the mist that condensed on the glass.

The other farm was a little run down but with good fences and a tidy barn. It was owned by a Canadian dairyman named Joe.

Joe's dog was all business and came up to Gunny in an expectant way, but Gunny snarled silently and the dog almost shrugged and marched up to help his farmer with the does. They unloaded quietly and money was exchanged and we loaded Julie back into the truck for the drive home.

Julie then started crying

"Oh, I could only cry in front of you because I know you'd understand. When I was in the hospital it was very hard. I really wished I would just die. But there are my girls and the farm. I have to keep trying."

I just listened for a while, wondering what to say. Julie had been so fit. The car accident had taken her neat athletic frame and twisted it down like a musical instrument compressed by something invisible and very heavy.

Finally I said, "You're the bravest person I have ever known. I mean, you're truly a courageous person. And you inspire us all. Look what you've accomplished. You built that farm up from nothing, and you're doing so well despite your injuries. We're all so proud of you. Your girls brag on you like anything. You make all of us better people."

"Really?" Julie said sniffing and then two things happened.

Julie's seat belt unsnapped and she fell into my lap.

I looked down at her, startled, and we hit a patch of ice.

The truck started to spin, and as I desperately spun the wheel to correct us, I realized that we had a cliff on one side that was a long cold drop into the black waters of the Sound.

"JULIE! Try to get off! You're blocking my brake leg!" I yelled.

Julie started laughing

"Ha ha. Brakes won't work! Hah ha, I can't! Ha ha ha! I can't move!"

Gunny decided at that moment to hide behind my back so I was now pinned against the steering wheel.

"Julie! My God, we're going to crash!"

"Hahahaha! What else can happen to me? I'm a quadriplegic! Sorry 'bout you! Hahahaha!"

I started trying to shove her up so as to free my legs but it was hard as Gunny was pressing into me from one side and Julie from another. She was laughing with joy, like a young girl jumping her first pony.

Outside the world twirled slowly like a kaleidoscope, and time condensed.

"Hahaha!" Julie laughed. "This is pretty bad! Hahahah Ha! It's a long drop down . . ."

Finally we stopped with a thump.

We had spun a bunch of times and came to rest against the flimsy guard rail.

I pushed Julie up and snapped her seat belt.

Gunny crept out panting.

"It's always fun to drive with you, Tea; you always cheer me up. Thank you," she told me.

"You're welcome," I said, weakly.

Then she said, "Lucky the goats weren't with us."

"Yes, lucky." I answered.

"You know, Tea, you are pretty brave too."

I turned to look at her face with bright eyes and crooked smile.

"I have a good example," I told her, squeezed her arm, then struggled to shift the Ford and drive home.

Julie sighed and turned to the window which fogged up with her breath. I saw her smile, a secret triumphant grin and she leaned forward and wiped the glass clearer with her cheek.

Slow Food

Pete and I get one or two channels on our TV set. They are public television and we have become enamored with the variety of fine cooking shows.

For one thing, the kitchens are extremely clean. The pots and pans and dishes are laid out in tidy and organized rows.

Pete is fascinated with all the new and strange gadgets that practically work magic on the food.

The chefs are a varied bunch. One is a Puerto Rican woman who is cheerful and vivacious. Another is an Italian woman who is practical and creates history while she cooks with her gloriously sweet and happy family.

One is an arrogant guy who tries to outdo other chefs.

Pete and I decided we should have our own cooking show. And it would look like this!

Tea and Pete's SLOW FOOD SHOW!

You would see our road leading up from the waters of the Sound towards heavy woodlands of hemlock and Doug fir. Our tiny cabin surrounded by fencelines of our paddocks and barn, then inside where an old woodstove is putting out joyful warmth, and retired sled dogs sleep on the worn and hairy couch. A falconry hawk sits balefully in the corner of the room on her perch and glares at the camera.

"Today Pete and I are going to show you how to cook lamb chops. Pete, will you get out the lamb chops, please?"

"Oh, of course, my darling. . . . Tea, the chops are still on the whole carcass. I thought you were going to break up this lamb yesterday?" says Pete.

"Oh, well, my dear, I forgot because the well went off and I had to carry water for all our livestock." There is a slight edge to my voice.

"Oh?" says Pete, "I will show our viewers how to break up this carcass."

"Good idea," I retort.

"First, I wash all our knives. Tea, dear, where are the knives? These are special knives given to us by Tea's brother, who is a marine. I think they're for warfare, but they work very well cutting up lamb."

"The knives are in the drawer, dear." I tell him.

"Ok, I'll get them out."

Pete pulls on drawer. It doesn't open. "Why won't it open?" He shoots a glance at me that the camera captures. You can tell Pete thinks it's MY fault.

He pulls harder, camera focus in on his face as he pulls with both hands.

"WHAT is caught in there . . ."

"The spatula thing and that whisk thing you bought," I tell him sweetly.

The drawer explodes outwards and utensils fly in every direction. We both gracefully duck dangerous-looking flying cooking implements.

Pete glares at me. He picks up dangerous-looking knives and washes them. Camera cuts to sheepdog scuttling from out of nowhere to grab a spatula and scurry away.

We carry the lamb carcass outside to our big cutting table. Pete washes the table.

Pete feels the carcass. You know, this carcass is still kind of frozen. He gives it a few hacks with one of the marine-man knives.

Some meat chips fly off. One hits me in the cheek and I flinch as it stings like hell.

"Ow! Watch it there, big guy. You almost took my eye out!"

Now the edge to my voice is very evident. Pete ignores me.

"Yep, it's very frozen. Well, we know what to do! We'll use the sawzall."

Pete quickly lays out extension cords and gets out a big sawzall.

"Pete, you must wash the blade first, my dear." I tell him.

"I KNOW!!! DEAR!"

He sounds a bit put off. The camera zooms in for a closeup of his face as he glares at me.

He starts the sawzall. The sound is deafening, we can barely hear him yell. "So now we must break up the carcass in quarters!"

The carcass, being frozen, flies off the table as soon as he puts pressure on it.

"It's very slippery," he cautions, then,

"Goddamn it! Tea, come here and help hold it!"

"No! You hit me in the cheek with a flying meat chip. I don't want to lose fingers as well," I answer.

"Son of a gun! Why didn't you thaw this god darn thing three days ago, it's solid like a rock!"

"Oh, just push on it harder." I tell him. "And don't yell at me. YOU could have taken it out of the freezer."

Pete's sawzall grinds to a halt, stuck in the frozen carcass.

"Chainsaw?" I ask him politely

A sheepdog appears out of nowhere and is licking up frozen chips of meat. Camera zooms in on dog.

"Oh hell! I'm just going to do leg of lamb, forget the stupid chops!"

Pete hacks off a leg with one of the big knives. The carcass rocks precariously on the old wooden table.

"There!" He slams it down triumphantly.

"Pete, it's still frozen. We have to thaw it," I tell him.

"Oh good God," Pete exclaims. "Well, why don't you show the viewers how to make cheese?"

"I don't want to now." I say.

"Why?" asks Pete.

"You're mad."

"I'm not MAD!"

"Yes, you are."

"You show them how to make cheese," Pete tells me finally.

"Ok, I will, but you have to milk the goat." I add.

"Nope."

"Why the hell not? I want my own show about knitting."

"Don't we all," mutters the camera man.

"WHAT! Look, Tea, the goats hate me; no milk comes out when I milk them. You milk them and I'll show our viewers how to make cheese."

"Oh, ok . . . goats don't like you because you squeeze them weird," I tell Pete.

"I do not." Pete says.

"Yes, you do." I whisper to him.

We walk down to the milking parlor area, sheepdogs following.

There are no goats.

"Uh, Tea, goats musta got out."

"I can see that."

"Ok, viewers, now we'll see how goats are rounded up in the deep forest with sheepdogs."

We start out down the road; dogs scout out ahead of us.

"Well, that answers one question," I say.

"Oh, what's that?" Pete queries.

"Why it's called SLOW food."

"Why is it called that?" Pete asks.

Camera zooms in on my face.

"Because it happens so slowly."

Camera zooms up above us and follows road to trails that spread out into dense forest. Miles and miles of forest . . . then fades to black.

§§§

Camera comes back on to show us two guys seated at Sporty's Bar and Grill in town.

A herd of goats pass by the window on the main road. Men glance at goats and continue eating. Camera focuses on their food, which is lamb chops.

Fade to black.

An International Run

The evening came as it always does in winter. It fell down like a cold hard hammer.

The rain had let up and my ewes were munching quietly. I had finished my last check and hurried back to our house to eat a long-awaited meal.

The opening of the front door revealed two things. Golden light from the old stone fireplace and my eldest son standing there looking at me with a phone receiver in his hand. His face looked distracted, but there was a trace of wry humor.

"Dad, it's the sheriff. He's at the Rosa's old place and I guess about fifty reindeer have broken out and are on the highway."

I look at this boy, six feet tall in jeans torn at the back where his pocket knife sits. A red flannel shirt a bit too small, his Christmas shirt his mother calls it.

He is black haired and he has his grandfather's eyes.

"What am I supposed to do?" I asked him.

Runner covered the phone.

"The sheriff wants us to help him, says bring a dog and round them up."

"Round them up? I don't think so. I think that's a job for Santa."

Runner gave me a look that only a sixteen-year-old boy can give his father. "Oh Dad! Ok, we'll be right down." He hung up the phone then added, "What dog will you take?"

"What dog? I think dogs in this case. I've never brought reindeer in before. I am not sure how it's done."

My youngest boy, Tod, appeared in a doorway.

He looked me in the eye.

"How 'bout roping 'em, Dad? I'll saddle Blue and meet you down there."

Runner gives his younger brother another look.

"You can't rope horned old reindeer."

"Why not?"

"Because, rope gets stuck on the horns, then the thing will ram your pony."

I stood deep in thought. Which dog?

I had an old dog, we called him Toady.

The old dog was lazy but wise. Big rough coated dog with calm brown eyes and eight years of work under his feet. He was a handsome black dog with a wide white ruff and a crooked stripe.

Our young dog was Mike, a big, slick-coated dog, prick-eared and almost all black. A fairly good work dog, although he was still only a year and a half.

My boy's cousin, Tsu, always called this dog Mike so the name stuck. I am not sure why, but somehow the child had taken to religion. And to her this dog was named after some biblical dog named Mike.

My family is not too biblical in the strict sense.

Not after the time Grandpa had told the local preacher that Coyote Old Man and Christ had similarities. The preacher had left in a huff and I guess he was offended by Grandpa's remark.

Although this so-called conversion of our youngest girl, through this biblical dog, made the preacher feel a bit proud. Old Grandpa merely winked.

My oldest uncle was scared stiff of Mike, our dog. Some problem he had with him in the woods behind our farthest pasture. Funny, as Mike is a friendly dog.

My house and my sister's house are two miles apart, and I wasn't surprised when Tsu, my niece, came in with Grandpa and they listened to the cousins explain the situation to her.

"Better take Mike, Uncle," Tsu proclaimed.

"He looks like a reindeer dog. And it's almost Christmas."

I called up Mike and Toad from the back porch. They followed us down to the old pickup and we all crammed inside.

It does snow a bit where we live and the landscape was quiet and silver, with snow on the trees and moonlight scudding its way between thin torn clouds.

We drove north towards town and sure enough came to a sheriff with tired eyes stopping traffic. Two cars and us.

"Oh hey, Frank. Thanks for coming. Think you can get these things back through the fenceline?"

I got out of the truck, followed by the kids and Grandpa, and switched on my flashlight and flicked it over the moving shapes 400 yards ahead of us.

The reindeer turned their heads, eyes glowing in the light. The closest ones spooked off a ways farther. Flighty, I thought.

Tsu pulled at my sleeve, "Think they can fly?"

My boys exchanged glances over her head.

I answered, "I hope not. Because my dogs can't fly."

"What do you think, Grandpa?" I asked my dad.

"I think they look tasty."

"No, about getting them inside the fenceline. Man, they have big antlers. Think they'd gore the dogs?"

"I don't know. I've only worked sheep and goats. Just keep the dogs well off, I guess."

I began to shine my light around the area to get a feel for the terrain. The highway here curved around next to a high cliff over the sea.

"Whose reindeer are these?" I asked the sheriff.

"Some guy from down South, his name is Steve, wife's name is Buffy."

I kept shining the flashlight to get a lay of the land and found where the break in the fenceline was.

The fence was heavy woven wire set on posts like telephone poles about eight feet high. I guessed it had to be high for reindeer.

Gates seemed to be all closed. A small hemlock had fallen on the fence and we would have to get that fixed.

The sheriff went to get a chainsaw from the back of his car.

"Well, before you start chainsawing and get them all spooked, I'll have my Tod walk up quietly and open that far gate. Then you boys and Grandpa can stand over there on that side and I can hopefully move the things through the gate. If they go through the gate and start to come through the hole, Runner, you send Toad over there to, God help him, head them off."

"What about Gunny?" piped up my niece.

"Tsu, don't get that pup out of the truck, why did you bring her? Want her to lose her nerve? She's only nine months old."

Tsu raised up a couple of inches, "She is NOT afraid of anything!"

Grandpa patted her on the shoulder, "Maybe not, but leave her in the truck."

My two dogs stood by my legs; both knew that something was up.

I decided to use Mike to get them through the gate and Toad to hold them from getting out again. I was worried if I started the chainsaw to fix that hole the reindeer would be two islands from here in a heartbeat.

I sent Mike way out, about halfway to the herd, and then I laid him down and sent him even farther out. This side of the road was a wide meadow running into deep woods. But something weird happened. Mike stopped dead, like he had run into a wall. There were shapes in front of him, but I couldn't figure out what they were. Bigger reindeer? Bulls perhaps. All the rest of the herd had run away from Mike pretty quickly, ankles clicking in the still cold air.

Mike was creeping up to something. When in doubt I always just used the dog's name. I kept shinning the flashlight and trying to make out what this was. The whole group of us walked quietly closer.

There was a large bunch of somethings. Very shaggy, they had all arranged themselves in a protective semicircle facing Mike.

The sheriff whispered, "What the hell are those things?"

The things were shaking their heads at Mike.

"Mike, Mikey, Mike . . ." I sang out to the dog so he'd know I was there.

Mike crept up and I could see now that whatever they were, they had the shape of a very shaggy cow. But these things were big. And the horns on their heads were upswept and sharp looking.

Mike looked definitely reluctant and turned back to look at me. I saw his eyes flash in the light.

"Dad, what are they?"

"I can't make them out. . . . Oh, Christ . . . Run for the truck!"

I picked up Tsu and all of us ran to the shelter of the truck and sheriff's car at the edge of the road.

Grandpa put an arm on mine. "Those are buffalo."

I shone the flashlight out towards them. Both dogs were facing the semicircle of buffalo.

We could hear the buffalo grunting.

"Oh, hell, I got to call my dogs back in. They'll get stomped."

One shape charged out and we could see smaller shapes, presumably the dogs, swarm out of the way, and then turn and stand again facing them.

I called the dogs, "Here dogs, here . . . that'll do Toad, that'll do Mike!" The dogs turned and ran back, glancing over their shoulders at the menacing shapes that surged up to follow them for a few yards.

In the truck Gunny was whining.

It was at that point my wife drove up.

She rolled down her window and asked, "Well, did you get the yaks?"

We all turned and looked at her.

"Yaks?" I queried. "Yaks? No, we are dealing with buffalo right now."

My wife smiled sweetly and put her hand under her chin, leaned on the window of the car.

"My darling, this guy has YAKS . . . and buffalo."

"Well, could someone call him on the phone! Why do I have to risk my life and my dogs for this guy?"

The sheriff then replied, "Because as soon as he heard his critters were out he was taken to the doctor complaining of chest pains."

Tsu then added, "He should know better. He should keep SHEEP like NORMAL people!"

"Quiet Tsu," Tod told her.

"Look, there are families around here. We gotta go get them in somehow."

"Well as a last resort . . . I could shoot them," the sheriff said quietly.

Grandpa said, "Look, I know how to get them back through the gate."

All eyes turned to Grandpa.

"Grandpa you are not going to try and spook them through. You are not going to try to rope them! That would be suicide," I told my father.

"Nope," said Grandpa. "Just go get a bucket of grain."

We all looked at Grandpa.

"Hum? Good idea," I said.

"I'll shake the can of grain on the other side of that fence and hopefully they'll hear it and come. But they weren't kept in that reindeer fencing, there must be a real big tough timbered corral or something somewhere. Go look for it, Marjean."

My wife said, "Ok." She drove off down the road to see if she could find a more permanent corral for the buffalo.

Tod went to the closest neighbors for grain. After we got a bucket, Grandpa went down the fenceline with the bucket shaking it and calling the buffalo softly. To our surprise they turned and all followed him.

My wife shouted from the road that she had found a big timbered paddock. So slowly they led the bison up the fenceline towards it. We followed in the truck. The tricky part was getting the buffalo into the paddock. No one wanted Grandpa to risk himself on the side of the fence the buffalo were on. And I didn't want to risk my dogs. So the boys went to other neighbors and got some flakes of hay which we tossed inside.

Grandpa crawled through the fence and shut the gate after the buffalo had walked in. Apparently someone had left it open and that was how the buffalo had gotten out.

We went back and got the reindeer through their gate and the sheriff and I mended the fenceline.

We were all pretty happy when we were done.

Then Runner turned around and said, "Hey, what's that?"

We stared hard for a few long minutes.

The sheriff then slowly replied, "It looks like an uh . . . ostrich."

Grandpa sadly shook his head. "Can't help with them, don't know ostriches."

Tsu piped up.

"I'll get Gunny?"

I sighed and looked at my wife.

"The Island is changing," I told her.

"Yep," she replied, "It truly is. And we still haven't seen the yaks."

The Meeting

The building was old, at least for a town as young as Seattle, maybe 100 years old. Big timber crossed and recrossed the lofty ceiling. Paint peeled in places and the wooden floor tilted and bent under our feet as we walked to our assigned table.

It was a growers meeting. Farmers from as far away as the Okanogan highlands came to meet the various people interested in slow and sustainable food. A lot of them were fancy chefs from the numerous restaurants of Seattle looking for the ultimate beef, cheese or chicken.

I had been called to go because of our unique sheep. The browsing of our sheep loose on the Island was starting to get out. And I guess it piqued the interest of the community.

I invited my friend Nancy, a clever and optimistic person who raises grass-fed beef.

Her simple pride in her beef was touching, and her tales of her foreman's interesting remedies were amusing. One time he had cured bloat with bluing.

Nancy decorated our table with an enormous exotic flower, crossed shepherds crooks, and a gigantic vase filled with many branches of pussy willows. The pussy willows made it difficult to move around.

We had to roll the vase a considerable distance to get it to our table and frankly, when we picked it up, I told her if we dropped it we would massacre people.

I had made flyers proclaiming the joy of our lamb. We had even brought one sheepdog. Little Cap slept under the table, behind the shepherd's plaid wool blanket.

People came and went. Two were farmers who discussed with me the merits of different sheep and our dogs. A few people asked about purchasing starter flocks or a ram lamb for their existing flocks.

One lady became enamored of Cap and bent over him, halfway under my table, talking to him and petting him. She asked me if I would consider selling him. She was a sweet lady from a wealthy suburb of Seattle. Of course I would not consider selling my Cap, but I had to ask her what she would do with a working sheepdog.

She told me he matched her living room perfectly. I shrugged at her and had to laugh. "No no!" I said, "I couldn't sell little Cap. I need him for my sheep. My advice is get a stuffed dog." She looked at me crossly and left in a huff.

Speakers at the podium talked about sustainability, compassion, lines at food banks growing. They spoke about the merits of grass fed, and about red cabbages and geoducks, raw milk and rye. It was amazing.

The lunch they served us was beyond belief. Nancy said she felt like weeping at the sight of home-grown food prepared by elegant chefs. The food lay in gleaming pots, smoking with steam. Lavish and rich scents came to us like an oasis in the desert. The scents held spices of every type and degree. One dish of simple parsnips could have started a minor war.

We were hungry and we helped ourselves to heaps of food, to the wonder of our more dainty appetite neighbors. After we had eaten we went back to our table. I brought a small plate of curried goat with onions; mushrooms decorated the top of the plate. I gave it to Cap, who promptly buried it under folds of the shepherd's plaid blanket.

Then chefs began appearing. Dressed in dark suits or in pristine white they came like priests followed by an entourage of helpers. One chef would talk to no one. He had a helper for that. He walked like an emperor and would approach a table, pick up a turnip. Caress it lovingly; put it to his nose for a delicate sniff, and then his helper would speak softly and earnestly to the grower. It was fascinating.

This chef, someone whispered to me, was a famous one from France. He was a guest chef at a restaurant in Seattle. He had grown up in a palace of chefs and could make dirt taste like whipped chocolate. I became increasing nervous as he approached our table. Nancy felt the strain to such an extent she left to get coffee.

My humble sign had a picture of lambs in the forest meadows browsing on salal. The simple words on the sign proclaimed that our lambs got to select the best grasses, herbs, and leaves just like in the old country.

The chef stopped before my table and carefully read the sign. He leaned in with his helpers and they all, slowly and carefully, read it again. The chef then turned to me. His helpers solemnly turned as well. He was actually going to speak.

My mouth was open, my eyes got big. I actually was a bit frightened. What was he going to say? That my lambs were too small? Not fat enough? What was he going to say? What?

He suddenly whipped around the table, pussy willows flew everywhere, and he grabbed me in his arms and amidst the gasps of the crowd planted a kiss directly on my mouth.

Then he held me at arms length and studied my face for a moment. Cap got up and looked seriously at him. The chef's expression held wonder and delight, a small child watching a wild butterfly or a swallow. He studied my face for long moments.

Then he let me go, reached into his elegant pocket and handed me his card. It smelled faintly of lemons, roses and lilacs. He then murmured to me like a lover might, his French accent rich and sweet.

"I will be calling you, for your wonder lambs." He told me with a look of deep affection. He then plucked a pussy willow bud, rolling it sinuously between his silky fingers.

I could only nod and smile weakly.

Then he turned with a swirl of helpers and strolled away.

Nancy came back with coffee and looked at my face.

"Whatever happened? Are you sick?"

"Oh no." I stammered, "I think I'm in love."

The Lift

———•———————————•———

Emily leaned her cheek against the bulkhead of the jet and felt the cold of the near window. Little drops of water that had raced past as the jet had taken off were now gone. Her reflection was a bit distorted by the two windows, thick to protect the passengers from the world at 30,000 feet.

She sighed and examined her face.

She was 35 now, divorced, no children. Her life was her work. The daily challenge of it, the meetings and travel and different people. It was one great puzzle to be played again and again. People thought her young-looking. Her face was touched by few lines and she worked out to keep herself fit and her energy high.

Her laptop sat on her tray and a message was looking out at her from her e-mail. It was from her current boyfriend. She tapped at it and read the message.

"Let's go to Costa Rica. Meet you there! Love you."

He had not signed his name.

Somehow that bothered her. Her cup full of ice was melting and she reached up and pushed the button to summon the flight attendant. He arrived and asked her what he could get her. She told him gin and tonic, and paid him. He brought it to her and she sipped at it and wondered why she was feeling this way. She examined her feelings, picking them up like shells on a strange pebbled beach. And the feelings lay in her hand lonely and cold and empty of what once lived there. She glanced back out the window and was surprised to see the beauty of the setting sun shining amber and gold on high cold mountains. She did not often see the sun set.

A baby cried from the seat in front of her. A man and woman were speaking softly to the child. It soon was silent, sleeping, she supposed.

She finished her drink and got up to get a pillow from the overhead compartment. Then arranged herself to sleep.

The woman next to her spoke. "Where are you from?"

Then without waiting for an answer she brightly continued, "I'm from Colorado. We raise sheep, my family and I. This is the first time I've ever gone anywhere. Went to Connecticut, my sister was having her first baby. A little girl! Seven pounds. She named her Agnes! Can you believe that?"

Emily looked at the woman, red curly hair, dark complexion, old jeans, a tired green t-shirt and worn cowboy boots.

Emily crossed her slim legs and told the woman "No."

The woman then tried again, "My name is Jean, as I said we raise sheep but we're starting a raw goat milk dairy. Have you ever tried goat milk?"

Emily wondered when this person would get the idea that she didn't want to talk to a stranger about farm animals.

"No, I drink soy milk."

"Soy milk? From beans? Huh? That's interesting! Any good?"

"Yes." Then Emily turned her face to the window and the woman finally realized that there would be no conversation.

I just don't want to get involved, Emily thought to herself.

She awoke to a great shuddering roar and had only seconds to realize that the jet was falling. She could see the flight attendant struggling to get the passengers to fasten their seat belts. She knew he was screaming at them but she could not hear him. It was very cold, hard to breathe. She looked at the attendant's eyes, at his expression, she drew it to herself the way a drowning person might clutch at a rope thrown to her. She saw in his eyes that they were dead already. Just living for a few more fractured moments, then it would be over.

She had flickering thoughts of Costa Rica, of Brian, her boyfriend. Then as suitcases and oxygen masks, and cups flew about her she could hear thin and high the cry of the baby in front of her and the prayers of the red-haired woman beside her. The woman took her hand. Then there was nothing, a feeling of floating, and a moment of heat. Then cold, then blackness. She then retreated, she thought into death, towards a strange cold shore with hermit crabs running back to the water like the drops of water sliding across the window of a jet taking off.

§§§

Junebug Robinson looked up into the evening sky and watched something fall. Like a comet it trailed earthward with red flames and great yellow golden sparks.

She thought to herself, "What the hell is that?"

The bright flaming ball grew bigger. As it fell she decided that it was closer than she thought. She could hear the twisting whine of engines. Then there was silence. And it fell in the quiet towards the far side of the next ridge.

Her eyes followed it and it still fell.

"Oh, God." Junebug said out loud to her sheepdogs. "It's a plane. . . ."

Her mind rebelled against the idea that in those flames were people. People falling now with seconds to live. The tree line finally hid the final impact, but Junebug felt it somewhere in her rib cage and she wondered what to do. She wished her husband were here.

Junebug was 68 years young, she would say to people that came to visit her. Or really to visit her husband's ranch. He had been dead seven years. Her husband had run dogs in sheepdog trials. He had been a very bright and kind handler. These two dogs beside her he had given her to use for ranch work.

Junebug had never trialed but thrilled to watch her husband work good dogs.

Junebug still raised sheep and was bringing a flock down from higher pastures to winter nearer their old homestead. She had with her the two sheepdogs, and her two livestock guardian dogs and a cell phone.

Her daughter made her carry the cell phone when out on the trail. Faith was perplexed by a mother that ran sheep in the mountains at almost seventy years "young."

"You got to carry it Mom, for me . . . for your children's peace of mind."

"Your brother doesn't worry," Junebug told her daughter.

Her daughter replied, "Oh the Marine, he's like you! That's why he doesn't worry. But I worry, and your grandkids worry. Please!"

Junebug flipped the phone open and was not surprised when she figured out it had no signal here behind one mountain pass.

"I'll call 911 when I get up high enough. There will be a signal up high. I'll go on towards the crash, since I'm the closest person. Maybe there are survivors."

Junebug climbed back on her old grulla horse and left the sheep, 200 ewes with older lambs. The dogs were edgy.

Her gift dogs, Nell and Glen.

Glen looked up at her. She smiled at him, old white-factored dog.

Nell was lying down pulling a thistle out of her plumed tail. She was a little rangy tri-colored girl with a joyful personality.

Junebug worried she didn't even have a first aid kit.

She frowned, probably no one had survived. But I have to go check, to see if I can help.

She urged the old horse forward and he, a veteran of the mountains, started down the trail with dogs following. They headed towards the ridgeline and the jet.

The evening was clear and she had checked the mountain's familiar peaks to give herself a direction. She knew these mountains pretty well. But she was off her normal trail and going cross country. The weather had been cold and there was a hint in the air of fall snow coming soon.

She thought of her husband for a moment, let herself sink into the sweet warm comfort of his arms, and his laughter and confidence.

Junebug could smell smoke.

§§§

Being dead was cold and confusing, thought Emily. She could hear the wind and it touched her and was numbingly cold. She then realized coming back to the surface of her mind that she had survived somehow. She was in pain and disoriented. But she couldn't move. She almost panicked, then realized, I am in my seat . . . I am strapped in my seat. She glanced up. She saw her section of jet seats and floor but nothing over her head but sky. The red-haired woman whose hand she had been holding when they crashed was gone, and that brought Emily up sharp, she swallowed and felt her heart race in her chest.

She had once been to a funeral. Closed coffin. "No, I do not want to see a dead person. I want to remember what they were like in real life."

She remembered herself saying that. A few tears ran down her cheeks to sting in cuts on her face as she thought of the woman's hand, so warm and fragile in her own. She hadn't talked to the woman about her goats and raw milk dairy and now that woman was gone. "I was the last person who talked to her. And I wouldn't even talk to her about her goats." Emily thought, she felt like her heart was breaking over that simple fact.

She struggled but could not get out of her seat. She fumbled for the seat belt buckle and it wouldn't open. Bent maybe . . .

She heard a noise. A soft groan. Then clearly a baby. The baby whimpered, a little kitten mewling sound. Then as it gathered strength, and perhaps awareness that wherever it was Mom was not nearby and that means bad things to any small baby, it began to squall.

Emily fought the seat belt. But it would not release. She gave up. She had never experienced cold like this. The tips of her fingers and feet were throbbing, aching from the cold. Moments came to her memory: standing outside the opera house with her boyfriend. They laughed and their breath made clouds in the air. She remembered seeing a man walk by, rubbing his gloveless hands briskly.

She began to yell, and then scream for help. She could smell smoke and jet fuel. She could see patches of flickering red, what was left of the jet's fuselage. It was still burning.

Then she was quiet and stopped struggling. The baby, however, went on crying, a broken and desperate sound.

She heard the groan again and with a kind of shocked horror saw that it came from a man who was crawling towards her.

She could see he was injured. He crawled with a determined look on his face.

Sometimes he would stop, focusing inwards and feeling along his side and it was then that he would groan softly. She wanted to look away but did not. No one can be hurt like that? Can they?

He was coming towards her. In his hand was a pocket knife.

Emily had a long time to watch him crawl. He was dressed in clothes that were fashionable with young people that liked the outdoors, clothes that she herself would never wear.

He looked Hispanic and his golden skin and black hair were matted with blood.

His face was set with an expression of determination. She detached herself from her situation and was able to compare his expression to someone trying to pass the Bar or someone who is driving his pregnant wife to the hospital.

He never spoke to her although his eyes were locked on hers.

When he finally reached her, he began slowly, patiently, delicately, sawing away at the seat belt.

They never spoke. The baby still cried into the night for hands to comfort it, for food and warmth, what all babies need. "Where are you?" the baby cried, "I am here and in big trouble, come get me!"

The man sawed away, but Emily could tell that he was becoming weaker. Finally the belt parted and Emily fell out of her seat to the ground, almost unable to move from the cold.

The man slumped forward and she reached out to him and saw the great pool of blood that he had trailed behind him. He was dead.

Part of Emily wanted just to be practical. Part of her wanted to scream bloody murder at the horror of this moment. Part of her said, "Wake up, Wake up this is a dream . . . a dream . . . you are in Costa Rica. Wake up."

The baby drew air into her outraged lungs and bawled.

Emily took the pocket knife from the man's hand and was so disorientated that she patted him briefly on the shoulder. As she might have patted a trusted subordinate at work. But she meant it sincerely. "Thank you . . . I don't know your name. Thank you."

Then she struggled to her feet. Her shoes were gone. She remembered the airline attendant telling them to remove their shoes. Her feet were now numb. She got up and looked at herself. She was still in the dress and slip she had put on that morning, long ago in her apartment in New York.

She smoothed her dress. Her nylons were torn and she looked around for the overhead compartment to get her coat. But there was no plane. She was standing in an opening. "What do you call them?" She thought briefly, a meadow. She was standing in a meadow in a forest on a mountainside.

She decided what to do. She walked towards the crying baby. Overhead clouds scudded.

The baby was strapped to her seat and taking great breaths of air and turning them into a sound that split the frozen night. Her cheeks were a dusky rose, her hair, what little she had, was tied in sweet little knots of ribbons.

She seemed unhurt except for the cold.

Emily fumbled with the baby's straps and then caught the little girl up to her breast. She murmured what she knew to be the right words, soft gentle comforting sounds. Emily breathed in the sweet smell of powder and lotion that had been rubbed on this child by loving hands that were now gone.

The baby did not know whose hands held her. But she could sense that here was a friend in a bad place and soon was quiet although trembling with cold.

Emily looked around herself. Now what do I do? She looked at the little baby girl. On her bib was embroidered by hand the name Yvonne.

§§§

The burning patches from the jet wreckage were big. Junebug was nervous. The jet fuel smell and acrid smoke were powerful in the air. Her horse breathed deeply and his ears were pricked. But he tried to be brave and confident because of June.

June tried to be brave because of her memories.

She remembered her husband driving over icy passes with the stock truck and trailer, laughing at her fears.

She remembered his hand over hers as they sat next to a hospital bed with their son lying there so still from a motorcycle accident. He had squeezed her hand and stroked her cheek with one rough finger.

"It will be ok," he had whispered.

Junebug told the horse, "We can do this, easy Smoke." The horse stopped. There was the nose of the jet, blackened and charred but still recognizable.

Junebug muttered a quick prayer that she halfway believed. And went on.

§§§

Emily staggered towards the part of the plane that was burning. She could smell the jet fuel but here was heat and without warmth she felt she would die. She got as close as she could and tried not to look for anything human in the wreckage. The baby's shivering grew less. Emily sat down on a piece of metal thrown off the plane and tucked the baby closer in her chest.

She looked up. Someone will come, she thought. They will send out search planes. And tracking teams and helicopters.

She looked down at her bare feet. She was freezing. She had no idea what to do.

She lifted the baby away from her chest and began examining her. Yvonne started crying again but weaker and shook once. She brought the baby up close to her and the child struggled against her, stirring feelings of loneliness, loss and worry that overwhelmed Emily to such an extent that she felt faint.

Then she heard a sound, far off and faint. She raised her head. She heard a dog bark.

She looked around; the stars were coming out. The steel of the fuselage glittered in red flashes from the fires that illuminated the smoky ruins of the jet that lay all around.

She wondered what the dog was barking for. Was it a tracking dog? She didn't have any pets. She remembered her mother had a little white fuzzy dog. But somehow couldn't remember its name. Only its smell. As the dog had grown old it smelled bad and she often wondered why her mother had kept it. When it died her mother had cried.

As she glanced around she noticed things: clothes, suitcases, metal parts, and spills of liquid darkening the ground, plastic cups and a few shoes. The shoes drew her eyes. A child's tennis shoe, a man's hiking boots, a slipper. The idea that these were parts of someone's life was frightening. The barking dog got closer, then stopped.

There was another sound, a quiet plop, pud, scrape of something big walking towards her. Emily had no idea what it might be. She raised her head and looked in the direction of the sound.

I am dreaming, she thought.

It was an old woman on a horse with two dogs trailing her.

The dogs and horse and rider breathed out frosty breath, plumes to mix with the smoke from the burning jet.

The old woman stiffly got off her horse and dropped her reins to the ground. She walked towards Emily, her boots crunching in the gravel of the mountains as she came.

Emily closed her eyes. She heard the boots coming closer, crunch, crunch.

She held the baby closer. Yvonne whimpered once and tried to look up.

Emily opened her eyes and found that the old woman was kneeling in front of her and had taken both of Emily's forearms in her mittened hands.

"My God . . ." The old woman told her. "My God . . . you're a sight. Don't worry, here now, we will get you fixed up. My God, a baby . . . is your baby ok? Let me look. It's ok. I can only look if you let go of your baby for a moment. She looks fine. Just cold, but we'll fix her up. Just wait here while I get a blanket." The old woman stood up and shuffled back to the horse. She took off the saddle and came back with a wool blanket that smelled strongly of horse sweat. This she unfolded and tenderly wrapped it around Emily. Heat flooded her as the blanket had come right from the horse's back.

The old woman pulled Emily's feet and legs inside the blanket. And covered her head with her own wool cap. She put her mittens on Emily's hands. She took off her jacket and one wool sweater and wrapped her feet loosely in the sweater before tucking them back inside the horse blanket. Then she put her coat back on.

"Here now, this will start heating you up. You're cold and in shock. I can't do a lot about that right now, but I'm going to get you warmed up. I have to go up high and call 911 and tell them where the plane went down."

Emily grasped the old woman's hand. "Don't go . . . call from here."

"Oh honey, the cell phone doesn't work here. I'll leave my dogs with you for company. How about that? Don't move now, stay put . . . ok?"

The old woman peered intently into her eyes bright with tears. Emily nodded yes.

Junebug called the dogs. "Here Glen, here Nell, you lie down." The dogs lay on either side of Emily where Junebug instructed them.

"Now these are really special dogs, you know. They're working sheepdogs and they know many mountain secrets. They can keep you safe, just like they take care of my sheep. You just wait here with them. It'll be ok."

Emily nodded.

Junebug walked back to her horse, led him to an old stump and climbed on him bareback and then disappeared into the gathering darkness.

The dogs on either side of Emily did not move. But the female watched Emily's face, and her brown eyes seemed kind. Emily was a little scared of bigger dogs. But she took comfort that these dogs seemed so calm. She reached out her hand and stroked Nell's back. She wondered at the fact the dogs did what the old woman had told them.

"Good dogs." She told the dogs. Nell and Glen both wagged the tips of their tails, a quick flick. Her shivering was less and the baby seemed asleep.

Junebug climbed the nearest ridge and dialed 911 on her cell phone. Soon help would arrive.

She rode back down to the jet and searched for other survivors. There was no one else alive. She rode back to Emily and got off her horse.

"I got hold of 911; they'll be here shortly. Your baby looks fine, lucky she's a plump little thing. What's her name?"

Emily cleared her throat and answered. "It said Yvonne on her bib."

"She's not yours?"

"No. I found her here in the . . . wreckage." Emily started crying.

Junebug patted her arms and then hugged her, rocking her slowly.

"There. You'll be fine. It's just something bad happened to you. Let it out. It's all right." Sweet soothing words.

The baby awoke and started crying again.

Junebug softly took her up and felt her, looking at her intently.

"What's wrong with her? Is she dying?" Emily asked.

"Why no, she's just scared and hungry and cold. But I know just the cure for that."

Junebug got up and went back to the leather sack strung over the horn of her saddle, tossed on the hard ground. She pulled out a thermos.

Then she walked back. She poured a cupful of something that steamed into the thermos cup. And held it to Emily's lips. Emily drank it. It tasted sweet and warm and so good that Emily could have drunk it all.

Then the old woman took the baby and dipped her finger into the cup and again and again put it into the baby's mouth who sucked hungrily.

"The doctors will be mad at me feeding you! Doctors are all the same. But neither of you is really hurt. Just cold and sad, and scared. And this is the best cure."

Emily lay under the horse blanket and a feeling of calm spread over her. The stars shone, far off but friendly over them, and she noticed a great full moon began to rise.

One of the dogs yawned.

"What is that we're drinking?" Emily asked Junebug.

"Why, honey, it's goat's milk." Junebug told her.

§§§

The kid was a breech and one hind leg back. Emily had felt inside the screaming doe, then ran back into the old farmhouse and yelled for Bill, her husband. Twelve-year-old

Yvonne ran out of her bedroom. "He's at Rosa's fixing their tractor. What's wrong?"

"It's June, she's kidding and the kid is stuck bad! The vet is on vacation! Try to call Tea down the road!"

I got a call from Yvonne and, gathering up some lambing gear, jumped into the truck and drove to Emily's old farm. The barn was in the back and the straining doe in a clean jug. I knelt in the dark and scrubbed my hands and slowly inserted my right into the doe. I carefully brought up the hind leg that was back, then by pulling down and out with the doe's contractions soon delivered the big doe kid who lay gasping on the clean straw.

Yvonne began rubbing it with a towel. "It's so perfect!"

Emily patted me on the back and said cheerfully, "Thank you so much! That's my best milker! Bill will be so happy."

I smiled and said, "Well hold on! There are two more in there! Here, I'll show you how to sort out a tangle."

Emily smiled at me broadly and began to wash her hands in the soap bucket.

Then quietly she told me a story.

Pal

My second youngest brother is named Scotty. He is tall and imaginative with the soul and good singing voice of a fifteenth-century Italian poet.

When Grandpa taught all of us kids how to brain tan, Scotty sang Italian opera the whole time till we ganged up on him and tossed him into the dark cold waters of the Sound.

Scotty is still a bachelor. He falls in love easy and often, but he is very shy and will hardly say anything to a girl. Unlike my first brother, who is called elk man by Grandpa, till he finally married and settled down.

Scotty walks in awe of beauty.

He lives in a small cabin on a high open hill. In the fall and spring the fog creeps in from the Sound and surrounds the land like a twilit smoky sea. The cabin is a ramshackle structure and primitive roses climb on the porch and bloom at the first hint of warmth in springtime. Someone planted those roses a long time ago.

An old Scotsman named McLeod had lived there at the turn of the century and it was said that it was he who had brought the wild sheep to Bush Island.

He had died in the cabin, right after his wife had passed.

Both poor and sick during the great flu epidemic in 1918.

It was also said that it was he who had adopted my husband's family as he and his wife were childless. The old Scotsman had a journal and he wrote thoughts that came to him during the days of his life. Things like how lambing had gone and trailing the sheep down to the Sound to eat the seaweed there. One entry tells of how he wished he could get to the sales and how he met his wife, through their love of animals.

One morning Scotty came by our cabin to help me with lambing and milk goats.

Afterwards he and Tsu and I sit and talk. Scotty was downcast and he sat hunched and melancholy at our worn uneven kitchen table that rocked our cups.

"What's the matter, Uncle Scotty?" Tsu asked.

"My dog died, Old Frankie."

"I am very sorry," Tsu says to him.

"I'm moving cows on Saturday, taking them to the Toppenish Market for Sam, and now I have no dog."

"You can borrow Ta," Tsu offers.

"Oh that's sweet of you Tsu, very kind but no no, you must help here at home. I'll get by."

Scotty gets up, tells us goodbye and leaves.

He goes home to his cabin surrounded by fog. As he walks up the steep path through the mist and into sunshine blindingly bright, he sees a dog lying on his porch. His heart leaps up for a moment. But of course it isn't Frankie. He buried Frankie last Wednesday. This dog is black. Frankie was mostly white.

"Hey boy!" says Scotty.

The dog stands up slowly and looks at Scotty gravely. It's a pretty big dog for a border collie, with a thick wild coat and a wide white ruff of fur around his neck.

Scotty crouches down and strokes the dog's face and looks for a collar. There is an old leather collar on the dog made out of the rein from a bridle.

On it is cut the name Pal. The leather on the collar was cut almost in half at one spot, as if whoever put it there wanted the dog to be able to break it if he got caught somehow.

"Well, we'll call the vet and see if anyone is missing a dog," Scotty tells the dog.

Scotty goes inside. The dog follows smoothly. As Scotty calls the vet the dog lies down by the woodstove. He watches Scotty intently.

The vet has no reports of lost dogs.

Scotty goes to get the dog some of Frankie's old dog food. But the dog does not eat. He quietly watches Scotty.

Scotty rolls a ball for the dog, one of Frankie's old chewer balls. The dog watches it roll towards him and as it gets close he merely places his paw on it and stops it.

Scotty then sits next to the dog and tells him his troubles. How sad he is about losing old Frankie, and the fact that he has no sweetheart.

He pours out his heart and the black dog sighs and lays his head on Scotty's knee.

Scotty is silent for a long time. The scent of the new roses fills the room. He gets up, makes himself a sandwich and goes to bed early. He leaves the front door open in case the dog has to go out or go home.

The next morning Scotty rises early. The dog is standing waiting for him.

Scotty makes coffee and fixes his breakfast. He offers the dog a sausage. The dog sniffs it but does not take it.

The dog follows him outside and jumps into his truck as soon as he opens the door.

"Well, why do you want to come? Want to help?" Scotty asks the dog.

The dog looks out the window straight ahead.

Scotty shrugs, gets in, shuts the creaky Ford's door, and drives to Sam's.

Sam Takai has some land on the Island and raises crossbred steers. A few he hauls to market to sell. He is standing, impatient in the road as Scotty drives up.

"Hurry hurry, ferry won't wait, who is that dog? New one, eh? Hope it's better than your last mutt, that dog was a real coward. Rig's down there all ready for you to load."

Scotty winces, but he says nothing. Sure, he knew Frankie was a coward. But he was a good friend and he tried so hard.

Scotty shuts the door of the truck and somehow the black dog slips out. He stands there quietly.

Scotty tries to get him back inside. The dog merely looks up at him and starts panting a bit, then sneezes.

"Ok, come on, bet you lose me my job. Don't rush these steers or Sam will skin us both. I hope you know what you're doing."

Scotty walks to the corrals where the stock trailer is parked at the ramp ready for the cattle to load.

The steers are there, well grown and restless.

The dog slips under the fence.

"Wait, dog . . . darn it, wait." Scotty puts his hand to his face.

The dog circles back towards the steers and they turn and face him.

The dog stops.

Then the steers quietly turn and march one by one up the ramp and into the rig. Scotty can hear the sound of their hooves rattling the floorboards of the featherlite.

The steers stop and stand inside not moving.

The dog slowly turns and looks at Scotty.

Scotty is amazed. From behind him Sam says, "You train that dog, Scotty? You are one hell of a dog man. It took me an hour to round up these steers."

Scotty turns around and then is struck dumb. There stands Sam's daughter, twenty years old, as beautiful and wondrous a thing that ever stood in cow manure on the Island, slim and dark and black haired.

"Hi, Scotty," she says.

Scotty doesn't know what to say.

The dog goes up to her wagging its tail and she kneels and pets him.

"He's a good dog." She looks up at Scotty admiringly. Scotty thinks he might faint.

He can almost feel Bess's hands in his own hair.

"What's his name?"

Scotty gasps out, "Pal, he's lost, I found him on my doorstep yesterday night."

A twisty little breeze comes up and rakes the trees and spins loose needles from the Doug firs standing tall and silent all around. There is a faint smell of roses.

"Oh!" says Bess. "That's a good name. Pal! Pal!" she tells the dog.

Sam waves impatiently. "Ok. Go on now. Don't give them away like you did last time. Make some money."

Scotty shrugs and shuffles his boots and he and the dog get inside the truck and drive off.

The steers stand silent in the back, not a sound do they make.

It takes a couple of hours to get off the ferry and drive to the market.

He goes and gets his information and finds out when his turn in the auction ring will be. He fills out forms.

The dog follows him wherever he goes. Tail and head low, silent.

A man claps him on the back, Devon Lee. A big man with curly red hair.

"Hey, Scot, how are you, guy? Brought some of Sam's skinny old steers. Who is this dog? Man, he looks good. Where'd you get him? He a chicken like old Frank dog? See ya, Scot."

The man walks away before Scotty can think of anything to say.

He goes to watch the ring.

Livestock come and go. Some beautiful and slick, some old and some downright culls.

Men and women stand by and bid, hoping to lose a problem or make a buck.

Scotty goes to unload his steers. He opens the ramp, wondering if the steers will walk out or should he send the dog.

The steers are lined up facing out. The dog quietly slips by them to the back of the rig and under the watchful amber eyes of the black dog they march out into the holding pen to wait their turn.

They go into the ring. And bidding begins.

At first Scotty is worried. Sam's stock doesn't usually sell well.

But the steers make some good bids and Scotty smiles and touches Pal's cool furred head.

Later the market manager pays Scotty and he walks back to the rig and the dog follows him then stops.

There is a man standing near the rig. He is tall with dark curly hair and grey eyes set in a tanned and reddened face. He is wearing canvas pants and an old torn wool sweater.

The dog goes up to him and turns and lies down at his feet. They both watch Scotty.

The man puts his hand down and strokes the dog's head once.

He smiles at Scotty, puts a work hardened hand to his brow as if to tip his hat, and then turns quietly away and walks off down the dusty road that leads back home towards the Island. The dog trails him.

Scotty gets a strange feeling in the pit of his stomach, he can smell faintly the hint of new roses. He asks a man standing near, "Who is that guy? I've never seen him here before."

The man looks at him blankly. "What guy?" Then he walks off as well.

Scotty goes home.

Sam is so happy with the money Scotty got for the steers he gives Scotty a $20 dollar bill and permission to take Bess out. Sam is very old fashioned.

Bess and Scotty go to the movie theatre.

Later that next day, Scotty tells us this story.

§§§

Years later while throwing out some old things we find the old Scotsman's journal. And there on the opening page is a faded dry rose, crumbling to dust as we touch it, from the front porch of the cabin and this dedication.

♠ T Yamamoto ♠

For Pal and Sally

Who spoke without words.

Worked without pay

Loved fully and deep

And are buried here

In a faraway land.

The Afterlife With Dogs

"Whoa, hell! This thing is slippery."

Caleb stood on a rainbow and below his shaky boots were thunderheads, dark and menacing. He took one step at a time; his work boots were slick as he spent more time on horseback than he walked. He crept carefully southwards towards a far green country he could see in the distance. He thought he could hear dogs barking.

"I'm dreaming," he told himself. "But I'll do what my mother said was the best thing for adventurous dreams. Go with it . . . so I'm going." The last thing he had remembered was seeing his dog Bronco get tossed by a bull. Then his little horse turned and the bull caught Smoke on the flank and flipped him like a tin can. Caleb remembered regretting his life for those few stretched-out seconds. His life had been lonely, except for Bronco and his pony. He saw his past flash across his mind, seconds that lingered and stung like sweat in a cut. He wished he had asked Mary to be his wife. He wished he'd been at the farm when his Granny had died of T.B. instead of trailing cattle.

But now he was here, wherever this was.

He walked carefully on and thunder clapped and roared beneath him and lightening flashed.

He bent down and felt the thing he was gingerly walking on, "What the hell is it?" he wondered aloud, it was slick as ice and as warm as summer, and lit up like many emeralds, rubies and topazes, diamonds and sapphires had been liquefied and run together and poured into a graceful arch. He stood back up.

Caleb squinted and stared at what appeared to be a person in the distance standing on that green shore, wearing a pale robe, smiling peacefully at him. All kinds of animals surrounded this person. A lot of them were dogs. The person had wings. The wings were dark golden like those of an eagle. The wings flapped once and the figure rose a few feet off the ground. Caleb supposed it was trying to get a better view of him.

He finally arrived on solid ground and tipped his hat at the figure with wings, then turned to look at what he had just crossed over.

It was a bridge made out of the light of a thousand rainbows.

"Greetings, Cowboy," said the angel. "Welcome. Here you are after walking across the shadow lands to find your beloved pet."

Caleb squinted, "My what? Uh . . . Sir . . . Ma'am?"

"Why your pet, there he is." The angel pointed a long bronze finger and there was Bronco staring at him like he had never been crushed by that bull.

"Well, I'll be damned," Caleb said.

The angel nodded and smiled.

Caleb called out, "Bronco get your sorry ass over here, what the hell you doing leaving me like that?"

Bronco, a black slick-coated McNab trotted obediently over to Caleb's feet.

Caleb knelt down and roughed his head a bit in his version of a caress.

"Ok, Bronco, let's go." Caleb turned back to the bridge.

"Wait, Cowboy!" said the musical voice of the angel. "Sir, you're dead and so is your dog. This is where you meet your beloved pet and then go on into heaven. You cannot leave," the angel told him.

Caleb turned. "What the hell? Screw you Mister or Miss, begging your pardon. I'm not staying here! This place gives me the creeps. I'm leaving with my dog, so get your fluttery self outta my way." The angel had flown over, barring his path to the bridge.

"You cannot leave," the angel laughed, but there was a hint of menace in the chimes of the angelic voice.

"Look," answered Caleb, "I have never been truly impolite, but if you don't get out of my way and let go of my dog, I'll rip those wings off of you and fry you up as breakfast just like a big quail!"

The angel had Bronco around the neck. The angel growled out, "Come on tough guy, let's go."

Caleb soberly told the angel, "I am afraid I can't scrap with someone in a dress." The cowboy suddenly trembled and he slowly pointed behind the angel's back.

"Look, it's Lucifer and all his minions from hell and a bunch of big corporations, come to set fire to your whole operation! FLY!"

The angel whipped around, let go of Bronco, and Caleb ran past. Bronco was right at his heels. His boots made musical ringing sounds on the bridge.

Caleb took off his dusty hat about halfway across and waved at the angel.

The angel looked at him, annoyed.

"What about your horse, Smoke? Don't you want him to be with you?" yelled the angel.

Caleb smiled and yelled back, "Nice try. But Smoke was pretty ornery, I believe Bronco and I will be joining old Smoke in that other kinda hot place. Where there is good whiskey and people are a bit more normal!"

Caleb turned and muttered, "Stupid angel."

He and his dog walked down the rainbow towards what sounded like a good bar.

He could hear a horse nickering.

Meanwhile, back on the other side of the rainbow, another angel approached the first.

"That was nice of you, Gabriel, letting him find his way to his own heaven."

"That's why I have the big wings." said Gabriel, tapping his head with one finger. "I use psychology."

We Remember You Still

————————————————————•

(For the Marine, his sheepdog, the little skinny dog in the desert, and the little girl in the shop window.)

His rifle was across his lap. But his fingers just touched the butt. His other hand was held out with a tiny piece of mystery meat from his MRE.

The dog took a tentative step towards him.

The Marine could hear the wind blowing, although muffled through his helmet. His sunglasses made everything darker and somehow that was comforting. Hot dust from the street blew by him in a pale stinging swirl.

The dog took another step. She was a little skinny street dog, brown with a bit of white on her chest, big wormy belly, and frayed ears.

This skinny dog made him lonely for his old dog. But his dog was on another continent, another time.

A world away.

His dog had always looked at him with love and trust in warm brown eyes. His dog had played with his daughter. His dog was buried at his sister's farm overlooking the ram paddock.

This dog had her tail tucked between her legs and every now and then trembled when the rapid pulse of a machine gun erupted a block or so away.

But she was so hungry and here was food offered in the hand of the Marine. So she stayed and advanced very slowly.

The Marine did not yet talk to her. He now understood the futility of speech. Instead he held out his hand.

The dog shifted her gaze slightly. The Marine was not staring at her directly but at the street. He could see Will's boot where it lay near the smoking ruin of the humvee.

The Marine thought of his own dog. How he had taken him to a rescue when he was deployed. How the woman there had promised him a safe home and he would be his again when he returned. But his dog had died and was buried.

The Marine swallowed. His throat was dry. He was thirsty.

The little skinny dog took two more steps. The food was right in front of her, inches away.

The Marine's will was still strong and his arm never wavered. If it had the dog would have fled. But he didn't move, and the old desert wind blew between them.

The dog raised her head and sniffed the air reading all that there was to tell on the scents in front of her.

Something old and trusting wafted into the dog's mind with those scents, a shared and beautiful past, ancient and unbreakable.

Finally the Marine spoke, his whisper so soft that the dog could only just hear it. "Shoka . . . shoka . . ."

The little skinny dog then decided, she took the last step, nibbled the food from the hand of the Marine. Then lay down beside him curled up under the rifle butt by his side.

And when his brother marines found him, it hushed them to silence. They approached quietly, with respect. The Marine propped against the wall, his hand still outstretched, whispering, and the little skinny dog standing slowly under his arm, baring her teeth at them.

They knelt down next to their marine, and the little skinny dog sensed that the men meant no harm. She curled back up under the rifle butt, pressed into the Marine's side.

The Marine finally put his arm down, a long way to earth. And it rested there.

One Marine asked another, "Shoka, what does that mean?"

The sergeant stood up, cradling his rifle, "It means, corporal . . ." He paused and looked out at the wrecked humvee, and the dusty shattered street. He saw a young girl watching from a shop window, her face wore a sad shy smile.

Bullet holes laced the window frame.

The sergeant glanced at the rooftops and then at the sky, a pale still blue.

He looked back down at the Marine and the little dog.

She wagged her tail a quick flick.

The sergeant then answered, "It means peacemaker."

The History of a Place

In summer I've been known to trail the sheep down to the rocky beaches to graze on seaweed at low tide.

One summer's day some kids, friends of Tsu's, came with me. They rode Skimmer, three on his old kind back, traipsing down to the water on a hot day, following the slow-moving flock through shaded trails and down the road where cars slowed in surprise to see sheep. My dogs followed the flock, panting.

Arriving on the beach, we sat and watched the sheep. The girls tired of asking Skimmer to swim, so they came and talked to me instead.

They pointed out towards the point where a big craggy boulder the size of a bull rose out of the now-shallow water. It had been dropped there by a glacier when the land was covered by ice.

The girls asked me its name.

"Well, Rayna the librarian told me its name was Ram's Jump."

Satisfied, they went to try to dig geoducks.

I watched that rock, standing in the calm shallow water at low tide. At high tide water swirled around this rock, treacherous and grave; during a gale waves rose around it like a hungry advancing army.

To swim out there would be perilous. But there were some who had.

§§§

1912

The ram was standing on a broad pinnacle of rock that peeked above the surface of the water. Waves crashed against the base of the stone and threatened to tear the sheep from his perch.

He stood there, back to the wind, with the stubborn determination of his breed. Horns darkened by salt spray, ears pricked as he looked at two men standing on the shingle 200 yards from him across water cold, dark, and deep.

Two dogs stood with the men. Both men were as different as the two dogs that crouched down by their feet.

Jaime McLeod was fair and quiet. His friend Roy was strong and dark, with a ready smile and a twinkle in his eyes. These two had known each for a long time, since Jaime had come to Bush Island bringing the sheep and his dogs. Roy's people had been here forever, and these two, ignoring the usual animosity of differences, became fast friends, each helping the other so both prospered.

Jaime sadly watched the ram and turned to his friend, Roy.

"It's the last of the sons of the sheep I brought with me. That wild goddamn ram! He would swim out there looking for seaweed when the weather was brooding, and now look."

They both looked at waves building by the power of wind and tide.

Roy said to his friend, "We could go get my boat and try to get him."

The two dogs looked up at the men. One was a big young dog with a thick coat of rough black and down-tipped ears. The other a tiny tri-colored slender bitch, with high white socks on her trim hard paws.

These two were a pair, the pride and heart of Jaime. He and his wife had no children, so they lavished their love on these dogs that helped them with the sheep. Roy's family accepted this behavior as normal for people of Scotland, as normal as fishing for salmon. Which both cultures did.

The dogs slept together in the old cow stall in the barn and where one was the other was not far behind. They had raised pups together and chased off a bobcat once.

The dog inched his way towards the water. Deep in his mind called ancestors on far high hills that told him to fetch this erring ram back to Jaime. The bitch softly whined, and that started it. The dog took off, ignoring the calls of Jaime trying to stop him.

He leaped into the water and began to swim. Jaime called himself hoarse, cursing the fate that was trying to take both his best ram and his dog.

Waves crashed over the dog as he swam towards the ram. The ram turned, wind lifting his wool and blew it in tattered skirts around his long legs.

When the dog reached the rock, the ram swung down his head in challenge. The dog was at a disadvantage, being low at the rock base in the surging tide. The dog paddled frantically to either gain the rock or avoid being pounded to death on it.

The little bitch on the shingle watched and whined in fear and sorrow. Here was her partner, in trouble. Her heart broke and she ignored the desperate yell from Jaime, and scrambled past Roy, who reached quickly to grab her, and she jumped into the Sound and started swimming.

The dog had meanwhile made the rock and crawled towards the ram, murder in his eyes. The ram jumped high off the rock into the dark water which closed over his head.

The ram surfaced and met the bitch, who swung short around him trying to figure out how to fetch him back to shore while swimming. The dog jumped off the rock and began paddling towards the pair. Waves rose and fell; wind tore the heads off the waves and pelted spray in the faces of Jaime and Roy, who watched.

Jaime looked up past the swimming ram and dogs. His eyes widened and he touched his friend's arm. A high wild squall was flying towards them where the cold and warm air of spring met and turned the surf into a raging devil of confused waves flying every which way.

Jaime watched with abject horror as both ram and dogs disappeared into the tumult and then saw his friend kick off his boots.

"My God, Roy, what do you mean to do?"

Roy looked into his friend's sky blue eyes and smiled broadly.

"Jaime, you don't swim, but I'm Duwamish. I can't let your good dogs drown."

He then ran and jumped into the surf and began to swim.

There was no sign of either dog or the ram.

Roy swam strongly towards the last spot he had seen the dogs. He thanked his grandfather for training him to endure the cold of the water and wished for the fat that they used to rub on their bodies to protect them from the frigid cold that sucked life from your very bones.

Suddenly beside him up popped the bitch, struggling and choking as waves spun her over and under. He grabbed her by the neck and dove under one wave and then saw that the next one might be of use. He turned and the power of the water rushed him towards the shore. As he sped home, feet kicking one arm stroking the water like a knife, he saw the young dog break the surface and start padding like hell towards him.

They all fought the waves while Jaime stood on the beach, fretting and worried. What would he do if they all went under? As he had this very thought a wave came crashing down on the top of them and they disappeared in a storm of white foam.

Jaime tore at his boots and ran to the shingle and waded out, waves tearing at him.

The three surfaced again and Jaime heard Roy take a breath and glance behind himself, the next wave lifting them up and sweeping them towards the beach, where Jaime waited to grab them and help them ashore.

First he grabbed his friend's arm and then the bitch's scruff. He reached finally for his dog that stood shakily as he crawled up out of the water.

They then staggered to sit above the high tide mark, shaking with cold as they recovered as best they could. The squall line passed and the sun came out, turning the waters of the Sound to a deep and rich green.

The waves still tossed but not with as much violence, and the men and dogs huddled behind some high drift, in the sunlight.

Finally Jaime said, "Roy, you are by far the bravest man I know. Thank you. But," he added with a twinkle in his eye, "you didn't save my ram."

His friend laughed and spit out salt water. Then suddenly they heard it. They looked above them on the cliff and there stood the ram munching the new grass. He shook sea water out of his wool and it flew in glittering sparks in the sunshine, then he chewed peacefully, until he saw that murderous look return to the eyes of the young dog that then ran up the trail, closely followed by the bitch.

Jaime laughed and both men stood and swung around to follow the dogs.

§§§

I stand on the beach on a peaceful summer's day, letting the flock nibble the sea weed at low tide. And I hear the distant roar of surf, of the wind high and screeching.

The girls bring me back as one of them asks, "What are you thinking?"

I answer, "I am thinking about friendship, bravery, and luck."

Browsing Loose

We bring the sheep through the trails, narrow and winding. The tall firs over our heads are still, as it is a perfectly clear day in January.

I have a lot of clothes on, as browsing sheep is cold work. Mostly it is sitting and watching.

The sheep are lined up like peas in a pod down the leafy trail. They grip leaves and jerk sideways to pull them off. The ewes like the salal and evergreen huckleberry the best. A few lucky ewes find berries still clinging. These they eat with great relish. The sound of their chewing is comforting.

My little dogs are by my feet. Gunny is lying down, still and resting. Her eyes are bright and happy. Cap stands as he always does and watches the sheep with concern on his face. I do not recognize this till a few moments later.

The ewes move down the trail slowly, just nipping the leaves and moving on. The small herd of dairy goats stays close to me. One four-month-old kid has occasions of jumping around like a crazed cottontail and blunders into the dogs, who give her a look but leave her alone because of her youth.

Cap turns his head and looks down the trail. Old Skimmer, my horse, cocks an ear that way. He is ground-tied and standing on the trail with the ewes munching by him.

Cap's head comes up a bit. He is looking down the trail. He then glances at me. He cannot talk. But his eyes are telling me something is up. We are about two miles from home.

He turns back towards the trail and takes a few steps down it, then turns again and looks at me. The breeze moves the trees and then I can hear it, a tiny lonely sound, far away. Somehow as we moved the sheep down the trail we have missed a lamb.

She is crying for her flock.

Perhaps she was hidden in some spot in the paddocks of home and the dogs and I missed her. Or maybe she turned off the trail and wandered. The forest is deep and thick and it is easy to miss a sheep.

I am reluctant to move the flock as they have settled nicely in this spot. But we need to find her before something else does.

I position Gunny in the back and tell her to lie down, and she does this like a soldier. Cap looks into my eyes.

"Cap," I tell him solemnly, "look back." He turns and runs down the trail.

In my head I see him run, a little, wiry, white-factored dog. My little dog that will not head. Cap, who has health issues. He runs down the trails, listening for the lamb. Cap's hearing is not great, but I guess it's better than mine. The lamb must be somewhat close for me to hear her.

I cannot hear the lamb at all now, only that once when the breeze came up. Minutes tick by. Gunny lies still, not an ear moving. The ewes continue to eat, nip, jerk, crunch. One ewe calls once.

Suddenly Cap appears out of the darkness of the tree-shaded trail with a lamb in front of him. She runs towards her flock. Cap is panting. He then takes his place next to Gunny, standing watching the flock.

"Good dog," I tell him.

We move the sheep on towards the cathedral of trees and the only open land.

I have permission to graze here. The flock spreads out and looks for anything edible in the pale winter grass. I sit on Skimmer and give him his head and he too is allowed to graze.

An hour goes by in peace. The dogs stay by my horse, the sun is moving higher into the cold clear sky.

We watch birds. The robins are here looking for scant food. A Merlin cruises the edges of the trees. A daring, agile pilot, he zooms out and catches a robin, a bird almost his size. A single desperate struggle as they both fall towards the frozen ground, then silence except for the sheep moving and eating.

Cap is standing next to my horse, and he suddenly stands up taller. Gunny and I watch him. His hackles rise on his back. He gives a quiet ruff.

Gunny and I know what this means.

There is a loose dog somewhere. I pick up my reins and look around.

Far up the logging road a person is walking her dog, not on a leash, ignoring my signs that tell of the presence of sheep browsing loose here.

The person raises her hand to wave and her dog takes off towards us. She yells at him in vain.

I am alone, the flock in the open, except for my horse and two dogs. I pick up my reins and Skimmer spins towards the approaching dog.

I send Gunny round the flock to push them up the narrow trail at the entrance of the forest and out of the open. The wise ewes know that this narrow trail is their only chance. They run. The poor goats and old horned ewes and my mean ram at the back.

Cap, Skimmer, and I face the dog.

Gunny keeps the flock going down the trail. The ewes are running home, bells on the old ewes ring wildly. They are soon out of sight.

The dog is confronted by Cap, hackles raised, and Skimmer, who hates unknown dogs. I loosen the reins and grab the saddle horn as my balance is growing older.

Skimmer, ears pinned flat back, effectively blocks the strange dog, preventing him from racing after the flock. I pick up my reins, hoping Skimmer is not going to stomp the dog flat and dump me in the process.

Cap, angry now, barks and growls. The dog finally stops a few yards off. Looking at us surprised. It is a big feathered red dog. The owner runs up. She grabs her dog by the collar and takes off her belt and loops it through.

"Oh, I'm sorry; I guess he wanted to play. Sometimes he plays with the deer like that."

I sit silent on Skimmer and Cap is still growling. I can think of absolutely nothing to say to the woman.

Finally she adds, "I saw your signs but I didn't think you were around."

I still look at her and I cannot speak.

It is a gulf so wide that I do not know how to cross it.

Finally I turn Skimmer around and call off Cap and we go to find the flock, which are halfway home by now.

As we trot down the trails after my 40 ewes I am grateful that this has only happened twice in the years that I have browsed the sheep.

But there is a growing grief in my heart as I know the Island is changing, and like the spring tides and March storms, there is no stopping it.

When we get home, I put the flock back in their paddocks. They are fine. I look at my dogs and stroke old Skimmer.

I am grateful for this old partnership, like marriage, like church.

Outrun

The old woman was going through her memories. It was like walking room to room in her mind and knocking on doors that opened to brilliant sunshine or on days dark with rain.

Voices met her as she went from room to room and sometimes dogs barked or whined.

Her real bedroom door opened and the R.N. stepped through.

The old woman looked up.

"How are you today, Mrs. Brugio?"

"Well, I've not seen myself in the obituaries, so I guess I'm ok."

The nurse laughed and went to the old woman and took her pulse.

"Did you open the package from your granddaughter? Here. I'll help you."

The nurse put a big box on the bed and opened it quickly with lean, strong brown hands. Then she lifted the box towards her and let the old woman remove tissue paper from around the gift that lurked inside.

It was a stuffed dog, black and white. It was knitted and crocheted out of hand spun yarn and smelled faintly of hay and barns when the sunlight carries dust motes down like the glitter of heaven.

Mrs. Brugio stroked it. "How fine this is."

The nurse smiled. "A stuffed dog, how cute. Now you have a pet dog to keep you company."

The old woman looked up at her, a wise old serious look from obsidian eyes surrounded by a network of brown wrinkles.

"No, not a pet. All my dogs worked."

The nurse looked at the card. "Oh, this card says it's from your great grand-daughter. She says its name is Mike."

Mrs. Brugio laughed.

"Oh, I have heard of Mike!"

"Was that a dog of yours?"

"No, no. Didn't they ever teach you about the Sheepdog of God?"

The R.N. gave her a strange look. "Well no, I haven't heard of that. But I will ask my priest next time I see him."

Mrs. Brugio laughed again, "Ok, you do that!"

The nurse left.

The old woman glanced across the room towards the only thing that was truly hers.

It was an old chair. The seat was covered with what was once dark red velvet. The back and arms and legs were delicately carved with roses. And in the center portion was a herd of sheep with a shepherd and dog. One leg had chew marks on it.

Mrs. Brugio wished she could get out of bed to stroke those marks.

She closed her eyes and went back into the rooms of memory in her mind.

A dog appeared. She was a little black bitch with white tipped toes. Her hair was slick and shiny.

"Oh . . . there you are!" the old woman said to the dog in her mind.

The dog, tail wagging furiously, hurried towards her. The old woman, now weaving memory into dreaming, knelt down and stroked her.

"Do you remember chewing my good chair? I was angry at you and yelled and you went and sulked in a corner. Then I felt bad and carried you outside and petted you. You were only a pup."

The dog leaned against her.

"Oh, Ta . . ." the old woman muttered in her sleep, "Oh, Ta!"

Memories fluttered around her like swallows and she saw her old Grandpa and her aunt and uncle and the little cabin and sheep browsing the narrow trails.

The dog in her dreams got up and stared at her intently. And the old woman stood up as well and, surprised, looked down and saw herself a young girl with long light brown hair, wearing dusty jeans, and a hand spun sweater.

In the distance there were Bush Island sheep. And she could hear the little breeze in the tall firs and smell wood smoke from the old cabin. Distantly, she heard her aunt calling her.

"Tsu! Tsu girl, bring those sheep in! Supper!"

She looked up into the bright summer sky, then down at her little dog.

"Come on, Ta. Oh little Ta . . . Away . . ."

THE END

LaVergne, TN USA
22 November 2009
164992LV00003B/8/P